A GUY WALKS INTO A BAR...

A GUY WALKS INTO A BAR...

501 Bar Jokes, Stories, Anecdotes, Quips, Quotes, Riddles, and Wisecracks

MICHAEL LEWIS

Black Dog & Leventhal
Paperbacks

To Frank "Pop" Hetlyn (1929-2002)
One of the funniest guys I ever knew.
Whenever I saw you, you shared a joke.
I think you would have loved this book!

ISBN-13: 978-1-57912-452-6
ISBN-10: 1-57912-452-6

Library of Congress Cataloging-in-Publication Data on file at the offices of the publisher.

Book design: Cindy LaBreacht
Manufactured in the United States of America

Published by
Black Dog & Leventhal Publishers, Inc.
151 West 19th Street
New York, New York 10011

Distributed by
Workman Publishing Company
708 Broadway
New York, New York 10003

g f e d

Acknowledgements

There are many people who helped me with this project, and I'll inevitably forget someone. Please don't get offended . . . let me buy you a drink and tell you a joke!

Thanks and kudos to my family: Amy, Samantha, and Sydney. Now that I'm done with this one, maybe we can spend a few minutes together! (At least until the next book.) Thanks to great friends and supporters Marilyn Allen, agent extraordinaire and a real sweetheart; Laura Ross, my esteemed editor; my venerable publisher, J.P. Leventhal; Betty Hamilton, my mother-in-law and biggest fan; Stephen Spignesi, my frequent collaborator and Italian brother; great friends Lee and Janet Pfeiffer, who are always good for a laugh (often at my expense); Dr. Charles Berg, the world's funniest and most inspiring chiropractor guru; Ron Fry; George Hanssen; and the Hetlyn family—per capita, the funniest family I know.

Thanks to anyone who ever laughed at one of my jokes. Everybody should have people like Barbara Murphy, Kathy "Bunny" Kelly, Jeanne Etter, and Colin

Somerville around, because they laugh at everything and never remember a joke—so you can tell them the same ones over and over. Does wonders for the ego!

Finally, I want to thank anyone who contributed a joke to this book, especially Frank Hetlyn, Chuck Berg, John Birkner, Craig Borne, Franklin Dohanyos, Stephany Evans, Bill Foody, Mary Fowler, Gerry Giovinco, Lisa Hagan, John Hetlyn, Jean Naumann, Chuck Negron, Steve Spignesi, Pete Talamo, Darlyn Tillery, Steve Urbanowicz, Steve Wheatley, and Joe Zappulla.

CONTENTS

FOREWORD

**"The most wasted of all days
is one without laughter."
—e.e. cummings**

Maybe it's because I'm always trying to get laughs myself, but for some reason people frequently feel compelled to tell me jokes. Most of them I remember, write down, and retell. And many of the jokes I've heard through the years have been bar jokes. It's been a while since I've frequented bars ("married with children" tends to have that effect, I guess). So, to put this book together, I had to do a lot of research.

While writing and compiling, I came to one conclusion: A lot of funny stuff happens in bars! Inanimate objects talk. Animals perform. Those who have had one too many say some pretty rude things. People from virtually every country gather. Drinkers share tales of genies they've met and problems they're having at home. They share worldly advice and recount sexual triumphs. It seems that every denizen of every bar is looking to find solace and companionship along with their liquid refreshment; they all want some relief from their hectic daily lives . . . or, at the very least, they want to share a few laughs.

Within these pages, I've endeavored to collect, compile, write, and organize the largest, funniest collection of bar jokes ever. A huge undertaking to be sure—a veritable Magnum full of yuks—categorized by type for quick and easy reference. It is my hope that this book will provide a daily shot of humor and that it might even inspire you to share a joke or two that I might have missed. If you know a knee-slapper that I've missed, please write to me in care of the publisher, or e-mail me at SamsPop1@aol.com.

Caution: Some of these jokes are risqué. If you're offended by adult humor, well . . . maybe you need to take another drink!

"A hot dog and a hamburger walk into a bar…"

CLASSIC
ONE-LINERS

"My wife's idea of the four basic food groups is canned, frozen, freeze-dried and carry-out."

A hot dog and a hamburger walk into a bar.
The bartender stops them: "We don't serve food here!"

A guy walks into a bar. He says, "Ouch!"

Two guys walk into a bar.
You'd think the second guy would have ducked.

Three guys walk into a bar.
They all need stitches.

What's the worst thing about getting drunk in a bar?
You leave with Cindy Crawford
and wake up with Broderick Crawford.

Twenty-four hours in a day.
Twenty-four beers in a case. Coincidence?

Drunk #1: My wife drives me to drink.
Drunk #2: You're lucky. I have to walk.

Why was booze invented?
So ugly people can get laid, too.

I only drink on days with a "D" in them.

Two peanuts walked into a bar.
One was a salted.

BEER PRAYER

Our lager
Which art in barrels,
Hallowed be thy drink.
I will be drunk,
At home as I am in the pub.
Give us this day our foamy head
And forgive us our spillages,
As we forgive those who topple against us.
And lead us not into incarceration
But deliver us from hangovers.
For thine is the beer
and the ale
and the lager, forever and ever.
Barmen.

A guy walks into a bar and grabs a stool.
The bartender says, "What'll it be?"
"I'll be drinking till three . . ."
"Three what?" the barkeep asks. "Three shots?
Three beers?"
". . . A.M.," the man continues.

What's the difference between a drunk and an alcoholic?
Drunks don't have to go to those stupid meetings.

Did you hear about the new drink called a "card table"?
You drink one and your legs fold up under you.

A dyslexic man walks into a bra.

A pair of jumper cables walks into a bar.

The bartender says, "Okay, I'll serve you. But don't start anything."

A man walks into a bar with a slab of asphalt under his arm and says, "A beer please. And one for the road."

Did you hear about the cheap bartender? He hired midget barmaids so the drinks looked bigger.

SIGN SEEN IN BAR:
Beer nuts: $1.99
Deer nuts: Under a buck

Two antennae meet on the roof of a bar, fall in love, and get married at the bar. The ceremony wasn't so hot, but the reception was great.

Two five-dollar bills walk into a bar. The bartender says, "I'm sorry, but I can't serve you. This is a singles bar."

"A woman drove me to drink, and I didn't even have the decency to thank her."—W.C. Fields

Drunk #1: Why are you drinking so much?

Drunk #2: I donated my body to science, and I'm preserving it until they're ready to use it.

Two hydrogen atoms walk into a bar. One says, "I've lost my electron."

"Are you sure?"

"Yeah, I'm positive."

A neutron walks into a bar and orders a beer.

The bartender sets it down and says, "For you, no charge!"

Beer makes you smarter.

After all, it made Bud wiser!

An eyeball and a pile of dog crap walk into a bar.

"I'm not serving you guys," the bartender says to the eyeball. "You're out of your face, and he's steaming."

How do you know if the bartender hates you?
There is a string hanging out of your Bloody Mary!

Q: What do all men in singles bars have in common?
A: They're married.

A woman goes into a bar and asks for a
"Double Entendre." So the bartender gives her one.

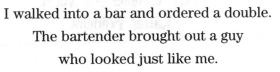

I walked into a bar and ordered a double.
The bartender brought out a guy
who looked just like me.

A bartender is just a pharmacist
with a limited inventory.

Q: What did the bartender say to his customers?

A: Your attention, please. Viagra now comes in liquid form. You can pour yourselves a real stiff one!

Why don't terrorists go out to bars?
Because they can get bombed at home.

"Give me a woman who loves beer
and I will conquer the world."
—Kaiser Wilhelm

Two cups of yogurt walk into a bar. The bartender says, "We don't serve your kind in here."

"Why not? We're cultured !"

A golf club walks into a bar and orders a beer, but the bartender refuses to serve him.

"Why not?" asks the golf club.

"You'll be driving later."

A brain walks into a bar and says, "I'll have a pint of beer, please."

The barman says, "Sorry, I can't serve you."

"Why not?"

"You're already out of your head."

A skeleton walks into a bar, hops on a stool, and says, "Give me a beer. And a mop."

A ghost walks into a bar at closing time. The bartender says, "Sorry, we don't serve spirits at this time of night."

Why did the fungi leave the crowded bar?
Because there wasn't mushroom.

A mushroom walks into a bar and says,
"Hey, could I get a beer please?"
    "No, I can't serve you."
    "Why not? I'm a Fungi!"

A number sixteen walks into a bar and
asks for a pint of beer.
    "Sorry, I can't serve you."
    "Why not?!"
    "You're under twenty-one."

A college professor walks into a bar.
"Bring me a martinus," he says

The bartender smiles politely and says,
"You mean martini?"

"If I want more than one,"
snaps the professor, "I'll order them."

An "L" and a "Z" walk into a bar.
The bartender yells, "Hey, get out of here!
We don't serve your type!"

Did you hear about the bar on the moon?
The drinks are terrific,
but there's no atmosphere.

SIGN SEEN IN BAR: Free Drinks Tomorrow

A guy walks into a bar wearing only Saran Wrap.

"We don't serve your kind here!" the bartender yells. "I can see your nuts."

I don't have a drinking problem.
I drink, I get drunk, I fall down. No problem.

What did the vampire bartender say?
"This blood's for you."

Don't trust volleyball-playing bartenders with your drinks. They might spike 'em.

Two guys walk into a bar and sit down to eat their lunches. The bartender says, "Sorry, but you can't eat your own food in here." So they look at each other, shrug, and swap lunches.

A ham, an egg, and a piece of toast go into a bar and order drinks.

The bartender says, "Sorry, we don't serve breakfast."

SIGN SEEN IN BAR: Don't drink and drive.
You might hit a bump and spill your drink.
And if you drink, don't park. Accidents cause people.

What's every man's favorite seven-course meal?
A hot dog and a six-pack.

Did you hear about the world's greatest drunk?

He's been in and out of Betty Ford more than President Ford.

Why is beer served cold?
So you can distinguish it from urine.

Beer: It's not just for breakfast anymore.

A Polish guy, a Black, an Italian, a priest, a rabbi, a dog, and a nun walk into a bar.

The bartender looks up and says, "What is this? Some kind of joke?"

A kid walks into a bar and says, "Got milk?"

"A drunk walks into a bar…"

DRUNKS IN BARS

*"I'm getting a second opinion
from Al's Bar and Grill."*

A drunk walks into a bar. After staring for some time at the only woman there, he walks over to her and kisses her forcefully. She jumps up and slaps him.

"I'm sorry. I thought you were my wife," he explains. "You look exactly like her."

"Why, you worthless, insufferable, wretched, no-good drunk!"

"Funny," he mutters, "you sound exactly like her, too."

Woman at bar (disgustedly): If you were my husband I would poison your drink.

Drunk: If you were my wife, I'd drink it.

Woman at bar: You, sir, are drunk!

Drunk: And you, ma'am, are ugly. But when I wake up, I will be sober!

A man heads for the bathroom, leaving his female companion standing at the bar. A drunk turns to her and says, "I really want to squeeze your tits. Will you let me?"

"How dare you! Get away from me, you sicko!"

Undaunted, the guy says, "Oh you have a beautiful ass. Can I rub it?"

"Look, you pervert, get away from me! When my boyfriend comes back he's going to kick your ass!"

The drunk plods on: "I want to stand you on your head, fill you up with beer, and down it in one big gulp."

"Okay, that's it!" Just then her mate returns. "What's going on here?" he asks.

"That guy right there said he wants to squeeze my tits!" Her boyfriend glares at the offending drunk and starts rolling up his sleeves.

"That's not all, he wants to rub my ass!" With that, her boyfriend takes a step toward the guy.

"And do you know what else he said? He wants to tip me upside down and fill me with beer and down it in one big gulp! Okay, now you can beat him up!"

Her boyfriend rolls down his sleeves, gets back on his bar stool, and says, "Sorry, hon. There's no way I'm starting anything with a guy who can drink that much beer!!!"

29

"When I read about the evils of drinking, I gave up reading."—Henny Youngman

A young woman nursing a drink at a bar is distressed as an unruly drunk sits down next to her.

"Say, honey. I'd really like t'get into those pants o'yours."

"Thanks anyway, but I've already got an asshole in there."

A drunk guy is sitting at a bar when a gorgeous blonde comes and sits next to him. After they each have a few drinks, the fellow says to her, "How about playing the Magician Game?"

"And what would that be?" she asks.

"We go to my place, have a few drinks, get into bed, have sex, and then you . . ."

". . . disappear," she says.

Two men are at a bar enjoying a few drinks, and they get pretty drunk. One notices a beautiful woman sitting in the corner and says to the other, "Wow, would I love to dance with that." His friend replies, "Well go ahead and ask her, then." So the first man walks up to the girl and says, "Excuse me. Would you be so kind as to dance with me?"

Seeing that the dude is totally drunk, the woman says, "I'm sorry. Right now I'm concentrating on matrimony, and I'd rather sit than dance." So the guy dejectedly returns to his friend. "So what did she say?" he asks.

"She said she's constipated on macaroni and would rather shit in her pants."

A woman is sitting at a bar, next to a drunk guy. The drunk says, "You must be single."

The woman is startled at his intuition. "Well, you know what, you're absolutely right. But how on earth did you know that?"

"You're ugly."

Old man Murphy visits the neighborhood bar every night for years. One day, he gets so drunk that he passes out into a pitcher of beer and dies. Considering he was practically family, the bartender thinks he should be the first to inform Mrs. Murphy of her husband's death. He goes to her house and rings the doorbell.

"I'm sorry to tell you, Gladys, but poor old Murph passed away at the bar today. He just collapsed in his beer and drowned."

Gladys begins to weep uncontrollably, covering her face with her apron. After composing herself somewhat, between sobs she says, "Tell me, did he suffer?"

"I don't think so. He got up three times to go to the men's room."

A very drunk man stands up to leave a bar and falls flat on his face. "Maybe all I need is some fresh air," he thinks, as he begins to crawl outside. He tries to stand up again, but falls face-first into the mud. "Screw it," he thinks. "I'll just crawl home."

The next morning, his wife finds him on the front steps, asleep.

"You went out drinking last night, didn't you?" she says.

"Uh, yes," he replies sheepishly. "How did you know?"

"Clancy's Bar called. You left your wheelchair there again."

A drunk walks out of a bar just as a nun is walking by. The drunk knocks her over.

"I guess you don't feel so tough now, eh, Batman?!"

NEW PROPOSED FDA ALCOHOL WARNING LABELS

Consumption of alcohol may...

★ make you believe you can converse cleverly with members of the opposite sex without spitting.

★ cause pregnancy.

★ cause a disruption in the time-space continuum whereby small (or even large) spans of time seem to disappear.

★ cause you to roll over in the morning and see something really scary (whose species and/or name you can't remember).

★ cause you to tell the boss what you REALLY think while photocopying your ass at the office Christmas party.

★ cause you to tell the same boring story over and over again until your friends want to SMASH YOUR HEAD IN.

★ make you believe that when you sing karaoke, you "sound just like the album."

★ cause you to shay shings like thish.

★ cause you to wake up with breath that could knock a buzzard off a dead animal from a hundred yards away.

★ remind you of some important things you need to say to your ex—who cares if it's four in the morning?

★ lead you to believe that you're tougher, more handsome, and better endowed than the really big guy at the end of the bar named Meat.

★ lead you to believe you are invisible.

★ make you believe that people are laughing WITH you.

★ make you wonder what the hell happened to your pants—and then decide it is totally unimportant.

★ make you think you have mystical kung fu powers.

Consumption of alcohol is...

★ a major factor in dancing like an epileptic.

★ the leading cause of inexplicable rug burns on the forehead.

Three drunks are sitting in a bar. Drunk Number One says, "I'm the bravest in here."

"Prove it," his soused friends say.

He puts his hand on the bar and tells the bartender to cut it off. The bartender reaches under the bar for a meat cleaver and—whack—off comes the hand.

The second drunk walks up to the bar and yells out, "Cut off my arm!" Whack! Off comes the arm.

The third friend stands on a stool and pulls out his penis. The bartender asks, "Oh, so you want me to cut it off?"

"NO!" yells the drunk. "Just rub it, it'll come off itself."

A drunk is staggering out of a bar with a fifth of booze in his pocket when he slips and falls. Struggling to his feet, he feels something wet running down his leg. "Please, God," he implores, "let it be blood!"

A guy who is already very intoxicated enters a very busy bar and says to the bartender, "Give me a beer, give everyone in the place a beer, and have one yourself."

The bartender smiles and proceeds to serve everyone a beer, including himself. He walks over to the benefactor, toasts him, and asks for his money.

"Umm, I ran out of money four bars ago," the drunk responds. At this, the bartender vaults over the bar and grabs the drunk by both his collar and the top of his pants. With one fluid motion, he delivers him quickly to the alley behind the bar.

The drunk pulls himself together and shuffles back through the bar's front door. He pulls himself back up on a stool and says to the bartender, "Give me a beer, and give everyone else a beer. But none for you. You're mean when you drink."

A drunk in a bar barfs all over himself. "Goddamn," he says. "I puked on my shirt again. If the wife finds out, she's gonna kill me."

"No problem," says the bartender, as he sticks ten bucks in the drunk's pocket. "Just tell her someone puked on you and gave you some cash to cover the cleaning bill."

So the drunk goes home and tells his wife the story. She reaches into his pocket and finds not one but two tens. "Why is there so much money?" she asks.

"Oh, yeah, he crapped in my pants, too."

A man has been hanging out in a bar all day, and he has to use the bathroom. He's in there for a while, yelling the entire time, so the barmaid reluctantly goes to check on him.

"Sir, what are you yelling about? You're scaring the customers."

"Every time I try to flush the toilet, something bites my balls!"

"Sir, you're sitting on the mop bucket."

A guy walks into a bar and sees a drunk slugging back shots as fast as the bartender can pour them.

"That's no way to drink good bourbon!" he tells the drunk.

"It's the only way I can drink it since my accident," the man replies, throwing down two more shots.

"Whoa, what happened?"

"I once knocked over a drink with my elbow."

"Always do sober what you said you'd do drunk. That will teach you to keep your mouth shut."
—Ernest Hemingway

Murray the drunk philosophizes to the bartender, "I have the secret to making a marriage last. Two times a week, the wife and I go to a nice restaurant. A little wine, good food, some conversation..."

"Really? That's the secret?"

"Oh, yeah. She goes Tuesdays, I go Fridays."

A well-dressed man walks into a bar and orders a martini. He hears mumbling and realizes that he's sitting next to a thoroughly drunk guy who keeps talking to himself and studying something in his hand. The drunk holds it up to the dim light and squints. The man leans closer to hear the drunk slurring, "Well, it looks like plastic." Then he rolls it between his fingers, looks at it curiously, and adds, "But it feels like rubber."

"What have you got there, guy?" Mr. Clean says.

"Damned if I know. Whatever it is, it looks like plastic and feels like rubber."

"Let me take a look," the second guy says. So the drunk hands it over. The guy rolls it between his thumb and fingers, then examines it closely, much as the drunk was doing. "You know, you're right. It's the strangest thing! It does look like plastic and feel like rubber, but I have no clue what it is. Where did you get it, anyway?"

"Outta my nose," the drunk mumbles.

A guy sits down at the bar and orders drink after drink in rapid succession.

"Is everything okay, pal?" the bartender asks.

"My wife and I got into a fight and she said she isn't talking to me for a month!"

Trying to put a positive spin on things, the bartender says, "Well, maybe that's kind of a good thing. You know, a little peace and quiet?"

"Yeah. But today is the last day."

Two drunks are sitting elbow to elbow at a bar.

"I wish I knew where I was going to die," the first one says.

"Why?" his friend asks.

"Because if I knew, then I wouldn't go there."

Did you hear about the world's biggest drunk?

He saw a billboard that read, **DRINK CANADA DRY**, so he went there and tried.

A drunk stumbles out of a bar just as another guy stumbles in all bloody and mangled.

"Call me an ambulance!" he shouts.

"Okay, you're an ambulance!" the drunk replies.

"It only takes one drink to get me loaded. Trouble is, I can't remember if it's the thirteenth or fourteenth."—George Burns

A guy walks into a bar and proceeds to order martini after martini. As he chugs down each drink, he removes the olive and places it in a jar he has pulled from his pocket. When the jar is finally full of olives, the man starts to leave.

"Excuse me, if you don't mind my asking," the bartender says. "But what have you been doing?"

"Ahh, nothin'. The wife just sent me out for a jar of olives!"

A man walks into a bar and asks for a beer. After drinking it, he looks in his shirt pocket and asks for another.

This happens a few more times: He orders, drinks up, then looks into his pocket, then orders another. Finally, the bartender says, "Listen, Bud, I can't help but wonder what the hell you're doing."

"I'm checking on a picture of my wife. When she looks good enough, I'll go home."

A man walks into a bar. "What'll you have?" the bartender asks.

"I'll have a beer and a shot of whiskey before the trouble starts."

The guy throws back the shot and chugs the beer chaser. He orders another round, then another.

Finally, the bartender says, "That'll be $22.50."

"*Now* the trouble starts," the guy says.

"Give strong drink unto him that is ready to perish
and wine unto those that be of heavy hearts.
Let him drink and forget his poverty and remember
his misery no more."—Proverbs 31: 6-7

A woman is sitting in a bar wearing a sleeveless top.
It appears she has never shaved her armpits in her
entire life—she has a thick black forest under each
arm. Every twenty minutes or so, she raises
her arm to flag the bartender for another drink.
This goes on all night. The other people in the bar
catch a glimpse of her hairy pits every time she
raises her arm.

Near the end of the night, a drunk at the end
of the bar says to the bartender, "Hey, I'd like to buy
the ballerina a drink."

"What makes you think she's a ballerina?"

"Any girl that can lift her leg that high *has* to
be a ballerina!"

First drunk: Did you sleep with my wife last night?
Second drunk: "Not a wink."

A bunch of guys are sitting around the local bar. They get pretty drunk, and the topic turns to Bubba, at the end of the bar, who is reputed to have the biggest dick in town. One of the guys gets up the courage to go up to Bubba and ask him how this came to be.

Well," says Bubba, "every night before bed, I tug on my dick and tap it on the bedpost three times."

"That's it?" asks the drunk.

"Yup," says Bubba.

So the guy goes home and quietly slips into his bedroom, pulls out his thing, tugs it, then taps it on the bedpost three times. His wife wakes up and says, "Bubba, is that you?"

Two airplane mechanics named Tom and Eric work at O'Hare Airport. Chicago gets fogged in one night, and Tom and Eric have nothing to do. Tom says to Eric, "I hear that you can get a buzz off drinking jet fuel." Since they have nothing better to do, they try it. Finally, their shift is over and they get to go home.

Next morning Tom calls Eric and says, "How are you feeling?" Eric says he's fine, never felt better. "Wow, this is great! We can drink all we want and not get a hangover." Tom says, "Well, there is one side effect, Eric. Have you farted yet?" Eric says, "No, why?"

"I did, and I'm calling you from Detroit!"

A man walks into his local tavern and sees that they've already decorated the place for the holiday season. Sitting at the bar, he notices his neighbor, drunk out of his mind, and he asks him, "Jack, do you know the difference between the baby Jesus and your wife?"

"No," replies the drunk.

"Well, the baby Jesus slept with a jackass one night; your wife sleeps with one every night."

John is sitting in his local pub one day, enjoying beer after beer and generally feeling pretty good about himself. Suddenly, a nun bursts in and appears at his table. "You should be ashamed of yourself, young man!" she cries. "Drinking is a sin! Alcohol is the blood of the devil!"

Getting pretty annoyed, John goes on the offensive. "How do you know this, Sister?"

"My mother superior told me so."

"But have you ever had a drink yourself? How can you be sure that what you are saying is right?"

"Don't be ridiculous—of course I have never taken a drink of alcohol myself."

"Then let me buy you a drink. If you still believe afterwards that it is evil, I will give up drinking for life."

"How could I, a nun, ever sit in this public house drinking?!"

"I'll get the bartender to put it in a teacup for you, and you can sit at that booth in the corner and no one will ever know."

The nun reluctantly agrees, so John says to the bartender, "Another pint for me, and a triple vodka on the rocks." Then, lowering his voice, he adds, "And could you put the vodka in a teacup?"

"Don't tell me!" the bartender yells. "Is that frikkin' nun here again!"

"When we drink, we get drunk. When we get drunk, we fall asleep. When we fall asleep, we commit no sin. When we commit no sin, we go to heaven. Sooooo, let's all get drunk and go to heaven!"— Brian O'Rourke

Three guys are sitting at a bar, talking about how drunk they got the night before.

The first guy says, "Man, I was so drunk I went home and blew chunks."

The second guy says, "Shit, that's nothing. I was so drunk I was driving home and got a DWI."

The third guy says, "Gimme a break! I was so drunk, I picked up a hooker and my wife caught us in bed."

"Hey, you guys don't understand!" the first guy explains. "Chunks is my dog!"

A drunk goes out to his car to go home for the night, but soon comes back in and picks up the pay phone to call the police. "Hello, occifers, they've stolen the dashboard, the steering wheel, the brake pedal, the radio, and even the accelerator out of my car," he wails. He gives them the name of the bar and agrees to meet the squad car out back in the parking lot, then goes out to wait.

A few minutes later, he sheepishly walks back into the bar and picks up the pay phone receiver. "Hello, police? Me again, the guy who called from Kelly's Bar? Never mind. I got in the backseat by mistake."

"Not all chemicals are bad. Without chemicals such as hydrogen and oxygen, for example, there would be no way to make water, a vital ingredient in beer."—Dave Barry

"I feel sorry for people who don't drink. When they wake up in the morning, that's as good as they're going to feel all day."—Frank Sinatra

A man has been drinking at a bar for hours when, in conversation with the bartender, he casually mentions that his girlfriend is still out in the car. Concerned about the cold, the bartender goes out to check on her. When he looks inside the steamed windows, he sees the guy's girlfriend passionately involved with another guy. The bartender shakes his head and walks back inside, then tells the drunk that he might want to check on her himself. The guy staggers out.

The bartender expects to hear yelling but, instead, the drunk walks back in and laughs. "That's just my buddy Dave. He's a stupid ass! He's so drunk, he thinks he's me!"

A man walks into a bar very drunk and asks the bartender for a drink.

The bartender politely declines to serve him, and offers to call him a cab. The drunk grumbles and staggers out the front door.

A few minutes later, the same drunk stumbles in the side door. He wobbles up to the bar and hollers for a drink. The bartender comes over, still politely but firmly refusing him service, and again offers to call a cab. The drunk curses angrily and shows himself out the door through which he came. Moments later, he comes in again, this time through the back door. He manages to drag himself up on a bar stool, gathers his wits, and attempts to order a drink. The bartender emphatically reminds him that he will be served no drinks, and either a cab or the police will be called immediately.

The surprised drunk looks at the bartender and, in hopeless anguish, cries, "Damn! How many bars do you work at?"

Three guys are sitting at a bar talking about their dates the previous night. The first guy insists, "My date must be a nurse, because she said, 'Lie back and relax. This won't hurt a bit.'"

The second guy concludes that his girl must be a schoolteacher, because she said, "Do it over and over until you get it right."

The third guy figures that his date must be a flight attendant, because she said, "Put this over your mouth and nose and continue to breathe normally."

A man is getting very drunk in a pub. He staggers to the bathroom, whipping out his penis even before he gets through the door. The thing is, he's wandered into the ladies room by mistake, surprising a woman primping in the mirror. "This is for ladies!" she screams. The drunk waves his dick at her and says, "So is this!"

Two old drunks are talking in a bar. The first one says, "When I was thirty and got a hard-on, I couldn't bend it with either of my hands. By the time I was forty, I could bend it about ten degrees if I tried really hard. By the time I was fifty, I could bend it about twenty degrees, no problem. I'm gonna be sixty next week, and now I can almost bend it in half with just one hand."

"So," says the second drunk, "what's your point?"

"I'm just wondering how much stronger I'm gonna get!"

A man in a bar has had one too many. When a beautiful lady sits down next to him, he turns to her and says, "Hey, how 'bout it, babe? You and me, gettin' it on. I've got a couple of dollars, and it looks like you could use a little money."

"What makes you think I charge by the inch?"

Three old guys are sitting at the local watering hole, discussing aging.

"Sixty is the worst age to be," says the sixty-year-old. "You always feel like you have to take a piss, but most of the time, you stand at the toilet and nothing comes out!"

"Ah, that's nothin'," says the seventy-year-old. "When you're seventy, you can't even crap anymore. You take laxatives, eat bran, and sit on the throne all day—and nothin'!"

"I gotta tell you whippersnappers," says the eighty-year-old, "eighty is the worst age of all."

"Do you have trouble peeing, too?" asks the sixty-year-old.

"No, not really. I pee every morning at six. I'm like a tall cow peeing on a flat rock, no problem at all."

"Do you have trouble crapping?" asks the seventy-year-old.

"No, same time every day. Six thirty."

"Okay," says the sixty-year-old guy. You pee every morning at six and crap every morning at six thirty. So what's so tough about being eighty?"

"I don't wake up until seven."

A drunk staggers into a bar demanding a beer. He argues back and forth with the bartender, who refuses to serve him. Finally, the bartender challenges him to get on the floor and do twenty push-ups to prove he's sober.

As he is doing the push-ups, another drunk staggers in. He surveys the scene for a minute, pokes the guy in the ribs with his shoe, and says, "Hey fella, I think your girlfriend has gone home."

It's closing time, and two drunks are getting ready to leave the bar. "God, I hate getting home at this hour. All I want to do is take my shoes off and crawl into bed, but Marge always wakes up and nags me for what seems like hours."

"Sneaking's not the way to do it. Try slamming the front door, stomping upstairs, and yelling, 'Hey baby, let's fuck.' When I do that, my wife always pretends she's sound asleep."

An elderly drunk man is sitting at the bar, crying in his beer. "What's wrong, guy?" the bartender asks.

"I'm married to a voluptuous, twenty-two-year-old nymphomaniac blonde."

"So what could be so bad about that?"

"I forget where I live!"

Three bums are hanging out in a dark corner of a bar. The first one goes up to the bartender and asks for a fork. He goes back to the dark booth. Soon, the second drunk goes to the bar and asks for a fork, too. Finally, the third guy asks the bartender for a straw. At this point, the bartender is wondering what's going on. "How come all your friends want forks and you want a straw?"

"Well," the drunk guys says, "my buddy Fred threw up, and the chunks are all gone."

Three drunks are hanging out at a strip bar. When one of the dancers comes over to dance in front of them, the first guy licks a hundred-dollar bill and slaps it on one side of her butt. His buddy licks a hundred-dollar bill and slaps it on the other side of her butt. The third guy takes out a credit card, swipes it through her butt crack, and takes the $200.

"He that drinks fast, pays slow."
—Benjamin Franklin

A man drinks a bottle of tequila every day. After years of putting up with his drunken behavior, his wife wants him to quit. So she follows him to the bar and sits down next to him. She asks the bartender for a bottle of tequila, then holds it up to his face. "I want you to see this. You see that worm floating on the bottom? It's dead. Now what does that tell you?"

"I think I got it! If I drink tequila, I won't get worms!"

Two drunk guys are standing at the bar getting their acts together near closing time.

"I've got an idea," says one. "Let's have one more drink and then go and find us some girls."

"No," replies the other one with a wink. "I've got more than I can handle at home."

"Great. Then let's have one more for the road and go up to your place."

A drunk guy moseys over to a beautiful woman at a bar and asks, "Would you be willing to go to bed with me for a million dollars?"

She's a little startled, but after a few seconds she says, "Yes, for a million dollars, I sure would."

"Okay then, would you go to bed with me for a quarter?"

Now the woman is angry. "Just what do you think I am?"

"Well, we've already established that. Now we're just haggling over price."

Three guys are sitting in a bar when another man comes in and starts drinking. After a while, he approaches the guys, and, pointing at the one in the middle, shouts, "I fucked your mom!" Then he goes off to get another drink. Ten minutes later he comes back, points at the same guy, and says, "Your mom gave me oral sex!" Then he staggers back to order one more. Fifteen minutes later, he gets right up in the same guy's face and yells, "I've had your mom bent over the kitchen sink!" At this point, they've had enough. The middle guy pushes the old man toward the door and shouts, "Look, Dad, you're drunk, go home!"

Joe is getting drunk in his local bar when a gorgeous woman walks in. Joe buys her a drink, then another and another. After some small talk, he asks her back to his place for a "good time."

"Look," says the woman, "What do you think I am? I don't turn into a slut after three drinks, you know!"

"Okay, so how many does it take?"

"I never should have switched from Scotch to martinis."—Humphrey Bogart's last words

Sitting at the bar, Rob is telling the bartender that he is drinking to forget the heartbreak of his broken engagement. "Would you marry someone who didn't know the meaning of the word *faithful*, who was vicious when the subject of fidelity came up?"

"No way! I wouldn't!" says the bartender.

"Well," says Rob, "neither would my fiancée."

A drunk guy approaches a cute girl in a singles bar. "Hi babe, how about a date?" he says.

"Don't waste your time. I never go out with a perfect stranger."

"Seems we're both in luck. I'm far from perfect."

A thoroughly intoxicated gentleman staggers into a bar and orders a drink. He soon notices a woman sitting a few stools down, and motions the bartender over. "I'd like to buy that old douche bag down there a drink," he says.

"Hey, come on now," the bartender pleads. "I run a respectable establishment, and I don't appreciate you calling my female customers douche bags."

"You're absolutely right, that was uncalled for," the guy says, ashamed. "Please allow me to buy the lady a cocktail."

"That's better," says the bartender, and he approaches the woman. "Ma'am, the gentleman sitting over there would like to buy you a drink. What can I get you?"

"How nice!" replies the woman. "I'll have a vinegar and water."

"Life is a waste of time, time is a waste of life, so get wasted all of the time and have the time of your life."—Michelle Mastrolacasa

A man sitting in a bar discovers that the front of his trousers is all wet. Turning to the man on his right, he asks, "Did you pour beer on my trousers?"

"Nope."

Turning to the man on his left, he asks, "Did you spill beer on my trousers?"

"Nope."

"Guess it was an inside job."

A man walks into a bar and orders a beer. The bartender puts a coaster and a beer up on the bar. Ten minutes later the man ordered another beer. The bartender brings him the beer and sees that the coaster has disappeared, so he brings another one. Ten minutes later, another beer, and again the coaster is missing. This time the bartender puts the beer down without a coaster.

"Hey" the man says, "what about my cookie?"

A wife is tired of her husband spending all his free time in a bar, so one night she decides to tag along with him. As they sit down, he asks her what she wants.

"Oh, I don't know. To get the full effect, I guess I'll have the same as you."

So the husband orders a couple of shots of Jack Daniels and throws back his shot. His wife watches him, then takes a sip from her glass and immediately spits it out on the floor. "Yuck, that's *terrible!*" she splutters. "I don't know how you can drink this stuff!"

"Well, there you go," cries the husband. "And you thought I was out here enjoying myself every night!"

A shy but drunk young man walks over to a beautiful girl in a bar and says, "Do you mind if I ask you a personal question?"

"Well actually, I do," she replies, "but I'm sure you're going to ask me anyway."

"How many men have you slept with?"

"That's my business!"

"Interesting! I didn't realize you made your living at it!"

A very drunk man orders a drink. As the bartender serves him, he asks him if he would like to try a game of darts. Only a dollar for three darts, and three in the bulls-eye wins a prize.

"I'm game," the drunk slurs, and he throws the first dart. It's a bulls-eye! He downs another drink, takes aim on wobbly feet . . . another bulls-eye! He throws down two more drinks, he's barely able to stand, but he somehow lets the last dart fly. A third bulls-eye!

Everyone in the bar is astounded. No one has ever won before, let alone anyone that drunk. The bartender searches for a prize, grabs a turtle from the terrarium on the bar, and presents it to the drunk as his prize.

Three weeks pass. The drunk returns and orders more drinks, then announces he would like to try the dart game again. To the total amazement and wonderment of all in attendance, he scores three more bulls-eyes and demands his prize.

The bartender has no idea what to give him, so he asks, "Hey, remind me, what did you win the last time?"

"A roast beef sandwich on a hard roll—it was great!" the guy replies.

> *"I drink to make other people interesting."*
> —George Jean Nathan

A guy goes into the men's room at the local bar and sidles up to the only available urinal, between two old drunks. He glances to his left and sees the guy pissing, but there are two streams.

"What the hell is that?" he asks.

"War wound. I took a bullet in the penis in North Africa. They were able to save my dick but I was left with two holes."

The guy looks to his right. He sees . . . three streams!

"What the hell is that?"

"War wound. Germany. Took a bullet in the penis for Uncle Sam, left three holes."

The two veterans then look over at the guy in the middle and see . . . twelve streams!!

"In what war did you serve?" one of them asks.

"Naah, it's not a war wound. My zipper's stuck!"

A guy walks into a bar. "Give me something tall and cold and filled with gin."

The drunk guy on the stool next to him makes a fist and says, "Hey, don't go talking about my wife like that!"

> "When I have one martini,
> I feel bigger, wiser, taller.
> When I have the second, I feel superlative.
> When I have more, there's no holding me."
> —William Faulkner

A man walks into a bar and throws back drink after drink, his hands shaking more and more with each swallow. Eventually, the bartender starts up a conversation with him.

"Hey Doc, what are you up to today?"

"Same old same old. Brain surgery."

A deaf guy walks into a bar. As he sits down, he writes his order in a spiral notebook he is carrying.

"I'm sorry about your handicap," the bartender writes as he serves him his beer. "How long have you been deaf?"

"About twenty-five years," the guy writes. "Tried all the hearing aids, and nothing did any good."

"There's nothing the doctors can do for you?"

"They told me to stop drinking."

"I guess that didn't work . . . ?"

"It worked great. When I quit cold turkey, I could hear everything."

"So what happened?"

"I liked what I was drinking more than what I was hearing."

"I haven't seen you in a while, Mike," the bartender says. "I thought you gave up drinking."

"I did, but I've been suffering from insomnia."

"So a couple of drinks help you get to sleep?"

"No, doesn't help the insomnia at all. But staying up doesn't bother me half as much."

A nearsighted drunk walks into a bar and sits down. "Hey Pat, who are all your friends?" he asks the bartender.

"Those aren't my friends," Pat laughs. "Those are my golf clubs!"

"Good, I was wondering how they all fit on one bar stool."

'Do not allow children to mix drinks.
It is unseemly and they use too much vermouth."
—Steve Allen

A well-to-do couple walk into a bar and sit down next to a drunk. Suddenly, the drunk lets out a tremendously loud fart.

"Excuse me! How dare you fart before my wife!" the man yells.

"Oh, sorry," the drunk slurs. "I didn't know it was her turn."

Night after night, a drunk in a bar sees the same guy walk up to a different girl, say a few words to her, and then they leave and come back an hour later, both smiling ear to ear. Finally, the drunk asks the guy, "Hey buddy, what's your deal?"

"I've seen you watching me night after night," the guy says. "I figured you'd ask. Okay, here's what I do: When I see a girl I like, I ask her, 'Tickle your ass with a feather?' and if she doesn't slap me in the face right there, we go out to my car. If she gets pissed, I say a little louder, 'Typical nasty weather.' She assumes she heard me wrong the first time, and then I just carry on a conversation. It works every time."

"I gotta try that," the drunk says as he stumbles away. He walks up to a gorgeous blonde and asks, "Hey baby, can I stick a feather up your ass?"

"What?!"

"Fucking rain!"

A drunk stumbles up to a woman in a bar. "How about coming back to my place for a nightcap?"

"That'll be the day!"

"Well, howzabout having dinner with me tomorrow night?"

"That'll be the day!"

"Okay, why don't we take my corporate jet and spend the weekend in Paris?"

"*This'll* be the day."

"Hey baby, can I buy you a drink?" the drunk asks.

The beautiful woman slowly turns and, in a slow southern drawl, says, "'Tell me, handsome, do you like sex?"

"Why, yeah, of course!"

"Do you like to travel?"

"Yes, ma'am. Yes, I do."

"Good. Then take a fucking hike."

"A horse walks into a bar…"

ANIMALS IN BARS

A horse walks into a bar.

The bartender asks, "Why the long face?"

A pony walks into a bar and says,

"Gimme a beer. I'm a little horse."

A horse walks into a bar and asks for a bit to eat!

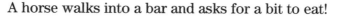

A guy walks into a bar and there is a horse serving drinks. The guy just stares until finally the horse says, "What's the problem? Haven't you ever seen a horse serving drinks before?"

The guy says, "No, it's not that. It's just that I never thought the ferret would sell the place."

A panda saunters into a saloon, sits down at the bar, and tells the barkeep, "Give me a sandwich and a beer."

"Sure, stranger," he says, and slaps a ham sandwich and a cold one in front of the creature.

The panda bites into the sandwich and chases it with a gulp of beer. Then he pulls his six-shooter from the holster, aims at a whiskey bottle behind the counter, and pulls the trigger. The bottle shatters onto the floor. The bartender is dumbfounded as he watches the bear return his gun to his holster and walk out the front door.

"Hey, what the hell is going on?" shouts the bartender as he runs after the bear.

The panda stops and says, "What did you expect? I'm a panda. P-A-N-D-A. Look it up." He then jumps on his horse and gallops off.

The baffled bartender reaches under the bar for his always handy unabridged dictionary. "Damn!!!" he mumbles. "There it is, in black and white, written by no less an authority than Noah Webster himself."

"pan-da—n. A large bear-like creature native to the mountains of China and Tibet, with distinctive white and black markings. Eats shoots and leaves."

A guy walks into a bar lugging an alligator under his arm. He puts the alligator up on the bar and says: "Attention, please. I would like to introduce you to Alan, my trained alligator. Witness as I open Alan's jaws and place my genitals therein. The gator will close his mouth over my apparatus for one minute. He'll then open his mouth and I'll remove myself, unharmed and unscathed. In return for witnessing this spectacle, each of you will buy me a beer."

The crowd murmurs in disbelief, and one by one they move in to get a closer look. The man stands up on the bar, drops his pants to his ankles, and slowly squats down to place his privates in the alligator's open mouth. The gator slowly clamps down as the crowd gasps as one. After a minute, the man grabs a beer bottle and smashes it on top of the alligator's head. The big lizard opens its mouth and the man removes his genitals—unblemished as promised. The crowd cheers, and everyone buys him a beer.

The man then stands up again on the bar, his pants still at his feet, and announces, "Now I'll pay $100 to anyone who's willing to give it a try."

A hush falls over the crowd. After a short while, towards the back of the bar a hand goes up.

"I'll give it a try," a woman says timidly, "but you have to promise not to hit me on the head with the beer bottle."

A three-legged dog walks into a saloon, looks around, and says, "I'm looking for the man who shot my paw."

A man walks into a bar with his pet alligator. He asks the bartender, "Do you serve lawyers here?"

"Yes, we do!"

"Good. Give me a beer, and I'll have a lawyer for my alligator."

A man walks into a bar with a duck on his head. The bartender says, "What can I do for you, sir?" The duck says, "Can you help me get this guy out of my ass?"

What is the difference between a dog and a fox?
About five beers.

A man sitting at a bar strikes up a conversation with the guy next to him. They get into a heated argument about whose dog could whoop the other's. They agree to come back to the bar with their pets and let them fight it out in the back alley.

They soon return with their dogs. One guy walks in with a mangy junkyard mutt; the other opens a case and lets out a twelve-inch-long purple dog. Everyone starts to laugh. Soon the purple dog beats the stuffing out of the mutt, takes a chomp out of the bartender's ankle, then runs off to kill every other dog in town.

As he's tending to his howling, injured pet, the owner of the first dog asks, "Where the hell did you get that dog?"

"The swamp," his opponent replies. "Before I cut his tail off and painted him purple, he was an alligator."

A termite walks into a bar and asks,
"Where's the bar tender?"

A man walks into a bar with his monkey.

He orders a beer and sits down to drink it.

As if on cue, the monkey goes into a squealing frenzy, jumping onto the Tiffany light, then onto the pool table, where he eats the cue ball.

The bartender shouts at the man, "Hey, did you just see what your stupid monkey just did? He ate the cue ball! I knew I shouldn't have let you bring that thing in here!"

"Good! I hope it kills the dumbass," says the man.

About two weeks later, the man comes back to the bar with his monkey. The wary bartender keeps his eye on them both. As the man drinks his beer, the monkey again goes crazy. He takes a maraschino cherry off the bar, sticks it up his ass, pulls it out, and eats it. Then he picks up a beer nut, sticks it up his ass, pulls it out, and eats it. This goes on with a few other items he finds around the bar.

Soon the bartender has seen enough. "Look at what your frikkin' monkey is doing now!"

"What do you expect? After that cue ball incident, he measures everything first."

A guy walks into a piano bar, sits down, and orders a tall glass of beer. He notices a blind man playing the piano. He has a mug filled with bills and coins on one side of the piano and a small monkey on the other, presumably to help him collect tips. The pianist starts playing "Your Song" by Elton John, and suddenly, the monkey jumps up on the bar and squats his ass down in the guy's beer. Then the monkey scampers back to the piano.

"What the hell!" says the guy, and he orders another beer. About three minutes later, the piano player starts playing Billy Joel's "New York State of Mind." The monkey again scampers along the bar and stick his ass in the guy's beer. "You little son of a bitch," he grumbles.

Soon, it happens a third time. Now the guy's really mad. He grabs the blind piano player by the shirt collar and says, "Hey buddy, do you know your monkey keeps sticking his ass in my beer!?"

"No, but if you hum a few bars I'll give it a try!"

A guy walks into a bar carrying a baby chimp in his arms. "I just bought this little guy," he tells the curious bartender. "We have no children and I didn't want to wait to adopt. He's going to live with us, just like one of the family. He'll eat at our table, even sleep in the bed between me and my wife."

"But what about the smell," the bartender asks.

"Oh, he'll just have to get used to it, like I did."

A gorilla walks into a bar, pulls up a stool, and orders a beer. The bartender pours him a mugful and says, "That'll be five bucks."

As the gorilla is paying for his beer, the bartender adds, "You know . . . we don't get many gorillas in here."

The gorilla replies, "At five bucks a beer, I'm not surprised."

> "I'd rather have a bottle in front of me, than a frontal lobotomy."—Tom Waits

A grasshopper walks into a bar, hops up onto a stool, and orders a beer. The bartender pours him a tall, frothy mug and says, "You know . . . we have a drink here named after you."

"You're kidding me!" the grasshopper replies. "You've got a drink named Murray?"

A duck walks into a bar and orders a beer. Noticing that he apparently has no pockets and is not holding a wallet, the bartender asks suspiciously, "And how do you intend to pay for that?"

"Put it on my bill."

A duck walks into a bar and says to the bartender, "Do you have any duck food?"

The bartender says, "Sorry buddy, no duck food here."

The next day, the duck goes into the same bar and says to the same bartender, "Do you have any duck food?"

The bartender says, "Hey pal, I thought I told you yesterday, we don't serve duck food."

The next day, the duck walks in, goes up to the same guy, and asks, "Do you have any duck food?"

"Look, you stupid duck," the bartender says, "I told you twice already, we *don't* have duck food! And if you come in here one more time asking for duck food, I'm going to nail your beak to this bar!!!"

The next day, the duck goes into the bar and says, "Do you have any nails?"

The bartender, a little surprised by the question, replies, "Um, no, I don't have any nails."

"Great! Do you have any duck food?"

A man walks into a bar with three little ducks and sits each of them on his own stool. He asks the bartender, "Could you keep an eye on my ducks while I go use the phone?" The bartender reluctantly agrees.

When the duck owner leaves, the bartender asks the first duck, "What's your name?"

"My name is Huey."

"Hello, Huey. How has your day been?"

"My day's been great. I've been slipping in and out of puddles all day."

Smiling, the bartender moves to the next duck and asks him the same questions. "My name is Dewey and I've had a great day. I've been slipping in and out of puddles all day." The bartender says, "Good for you! That sounds nice."

With this, the bartender moves to the third duck. "Don't tell me—your name's Louie and you've been slipping in and out of puddles all day."

"No. My name's Puddles, and my day sucked."

A guy walks into a bar and sees everyone crowded around a table, watching a little show. On the table is an upside down pot with a duck tap dancing on it. The man is impressed and announces, "I'm the owner of the Hamilton Brothers Circus, and I want to buy that duck! He's sure to draw a big crowd."

After some wheeling and dealing, the circus owner pays the bartender $10,000 for the talented duck. Feeling generous, the bartender even throws in the pot.

Three days later the circus owner storms back into the bar. "Your duck is a rip-off! I put him out there before a sold-out audience, and he didn't dance a single step!"

"That's weird. . . . Did you remember to light the candle under the pot?"

A penguin walks into a bar and asks the bartender, "Have you seen my brother?"

"I don't know. What does he look like?"

A penguin takes his car into a shop, and the mechanic says he needs about an hour to check it out. The penguin goes across the street to a bar to kill some time and orders a couple of beers. As you know, penguins have no arms, so he ends up getting the foam all over his beak.

When he finishes, he goes back to the garage and the mechanic says, "It looks like you blew a seal."

"No, that's just a little beer foam."

A baby seal walks into a bar. "What can I get you?" asks the bartender.

"Anything but Canadian Club."

A snake crawls into a bar. The bartender says, "Sorry, I can't serve you."

"May I ask why not?"

"Because you can't hold your liquor."

A very fat woman walks into a bar holding a duck under her arm. The bartender says, "Where'd you get the pig?"

The woman responds, "It's not a pig; it's a duck."

"I was talking to the duck."

Two pigs walk into a bar, get drunk, and ask, "Where's the bathroom?" The bartender points to the door and they rush in.

Two more pigs walk through the door. They soon get drunk and ask, "Where's the bathroom?" The bartender points to the door, and they rush away.

A fifth swine walks in. He soon gets drunk and then heads for the exit.

"Hey, buddy! Do you wanna know where the bathroom is?" says the bartender.

"No thanks," the piggy slurs, "I always go WEEWEEWEE all the way home!"

A man walks into a bar carrying a small pig, which he puts on the stool next to his. "A martini for me, and a scotch-and-soda for Percy, please." The bartender notices that the little porker has a wooden hind leg.

"What's with the pig? I mean, I've been tending bar for twenty-seven years, and no one ever brought a pig in for a drink."

"You don't understand," the man says. "This pig is very special to me. He's part of the family. He even saved my life."

"Really? How so?"

"One night we had a fire in the farmhouse and the pig came in and nibbled on my toes to wake me up. If he hadn't done that, I would've died."

"What an amazing story! And how did he get the wooden leg? Was he injured in the fire?"

"No. When a pig is this special, you can't eat him all at once."

A woman walks into a bar with a pig under her arm. "Where did you get that?" the bartender asks.

"I won her in a raffle!" the pig responds.

> "Always remember that I have taken more out of alcohol than alcohol has taken out of me."—Winston Churchill

A man walks into a bar with his black Labrador retriever and asks for a drink. The bartender says, "You can't bring that dog in here!"

"This is my seeing-eye dog."

"Oh man, I'm sorry. Here, the first one's on me."

The man takes his drink and goes to a table near the door. A few minutes later, another guy walks into the bar with a Chihuahua and asks for a drink. The bartender says, "Look, you can't bring that dog in here!"

"This is my seeing-eye dog."

"Try again, pal. I've never heard of a Chihuahua seeing-eye dog."

"What?! They gave me a Chihuahua?!?"

A dog walks into a bar, hops up on a stool, puts his paws on the bar, looks right into the bartender's eyes, and says, "Hi, there! Guess what? I'm a talking dog. Have you ever seen a talking dog before? How about a drink for the talking dog?"

The bartender thinks for a moment and says, "Alright. The toilet's right around the corner."

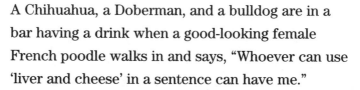

A Chihuahua, a Doberman, and a bulldog are in a bar having a drink when a good-looking female French poodle walks in and says, "Whoever can use 'liver and cheese' in a sentence can have me."

So the Doberman says, "I love liver and cheese."

The poodle says, "That's not good enough."

The bulldog says, "I hate liver and cheese."

She says, "Sorry, that's not very creative."

Then the little Chihuahua speaks up: "Liver alone . . . cheese mine."

A man walks into a bar and sits down next to a man with a dog at his feet. "Does your dog bite?" he asks.

"No."

With that, he leans down to pet the dog, who proceeds to snarl and bite his hand.

"Hey! I thought you said your dog didn't bite!"

"That's not my dog."

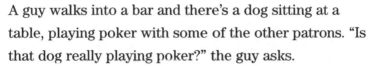

A guy walks into a bar and there's a dog sitting at a table, playing poker with some of the other patrons. "Is that dog really playing poker?" the guy asks.

The bartender replies, "Sure, but he's not too good. Whenever he has a good hand, he wags his tail."

Two drunks are sitting in a bar, watching a dog lick its balls. One drunk turns to the other and says, "Gee, I wish I could do that."

His friend answers, "I wouldn't advise it. I think the little bastard would bite you!"

A guy walks into a bar with his golden retriever. "Hey bartender, can I get a drink on the house if my dog talks for you?"

"Never seen a dog talk before," the bartender says. "But if you can prove to me yours does, I'll give you a drink. If not, I get to throw your ass out of here for wasting my time."

"Fair enough," says the guy. He turns to his dog. "Okay boy. Tell me—what is on top of a house?"

"Roof!" the dog proudly barks. The man turns and smiles at the bartender.

"Okay, boy. Now tell me—how does sandpaper feel?"

"Ruff!"

The bartender is starting to get fed up. "What the hell you tryin' to pull, mister?"

"Okay, okay," says the man. "One more question. Buddy, tell me—who is the greatest baseball player who ever lived?"

"Ruth."

As the man and the dog land with a thud in the alley behind the bar, the dog looks at his master and asks, "Do ya think maybe I shoulda said DiMaggio?"

A blind man walks into a bar with his seeing-eye dog on a leash, and immediately starts swinging him around.

The startled bartender says, "Hey buddy, what are you doing?"

"Don't mind me, I'm just scoping out some babes."

A guy walks into a bar, orders a triple Scotch, and drinks it down in one gulp.

"Wow," says the bartender, "something bad musta happened."

"I came home early today. I went up to the bedroom, and there was my wife having sex with my best friend."

"This one's on the house," the bartender says, as he pours another one. "Did you say anything to your wife?"

"Yeah, I told her to pack her bags and get out."

"What about your friend?"

"I did the only thing that came to mind. I looked him straight in the eye and said, 'Bad dog!'"

A woman walks into a bar, sits down next to a drunk, and sets her three-pound Chihuahua at her feet. A few minutes later, the drunk turns his head towards the floor and throws up. He looks down and sees the little dog struggling in the pool of vomit and says, "Whoa, I don't remember eating that!"

A guy walks into a bar carrying a small dog, orders a drink, and places the dog on the bar. The dog has no legs.

"What a cute little fella," the bartender says. "What's his name?"

"He doesn't have a name," the dog owner says. "Why bother? He couldn't come when I called him anyway."

A giraffe walks into a bar and the bartender asks, "Do you want a longneck?"

The giraffe replies, "Do I have a choice?"

A guy walks into a bar with an octopus. He sits the octopus down on a stool and says, "Folks, can I have your attention. This is Otto, the musical octopus. I will bet anyone fifty dollars that Otto can play any instrument you bring him."

A guy with a guitar walks up and hands the octopus a guitar, and the octopus proceed to play "Stairway to Heaven" better than Jimmy Page. So the man coughs up fifty dollars. Another guy brings up a trumpet, and Otto proceeds to toot it better than Miles Davis. So the man pays his fifty.

A third guy walks up with bagpipes. He hands them to the octopus, who fumbles around for a few minutes and finally sets the bagpipes down with a confused look.

"Ha!" the man says, "can't play it, can ya?"

"Play it? As soon as I can figure out how to take its pajamas off, I'm gonna fuck it!"

A man goes into a bar with a dog, sits down at the counter, and places the dog on the next stool. "Let me have a beer" says the man, and the dog says, "I'll have one too!"

The bartender laughs. "So, are you a ventriloquist or something?"

"No, he is a talking dog," replies the man, and the dog says, "That's right, so where's my beer?"

The startled bartender serves them their drinks and after talking with them a while, he realizes that they are on the level. Soon, the dog owner realizes he's out of smokes. Since the cigarette machine is out of order, he sends his dog down the street with ten dollars for a pack of cigarettes.

When the dog hasn't returned an hour later, the two men get worried and go out looking for him. Soon, they pass an alley and there's the dog—screwing another dog.

"I don't understand, Max," says the owner. "You never did this before."

"I never had ten dollars before!"

A guy walks into a bar with a giraffe and says, "A beer for me, and one for the giraffe, please." The two of them drink their beers. Then: "A shot for me, and one for the giraffe, too." And the two of them keep drinking all evening. Finally the giraffe passes out on the floor of the bar. The guy pays the tab and gets up to leave.

The bartender shouts out, "Hey! You're not going to leave that lying on the floor, are you?"

"That's not a lion," the man replies. "It's a giraffe."

A Polar bear walks into a bar and says to the bartender, "I'll have a gin……………. and tonic."

"What's with the big pause?" the bartender asks.

"I don't know," the bear says. "My dad had them, too."

A guy walks into a bar with a frog on his head. "Where did you get that?" the bartender asks.

"It started out as a little bump on my ass," the frog replies.

"The problem with some people is that
when they aren't drunk, they're sober."
—William Butler Yeats

A skunk, a giraffe, and a deer walk into a bar and order three drinks. All three animals chug them down instantly. They order round after round, obviously parched from a long day in the wilderness.

The three soon realize that they don't have pockets, and therefore have no money to pay their bill. Slowly, they try to back out the door before anyone notices.

"Hey, wait a minute!" the bartender calls out. "Who's gonna pay the tab?"

"Not me," says the skunk. "I only have a scent."

"I can't," says the deer. "I had a buck last week, and I'm expecting a little doe soon."

"They've done it to me again," the giraffe says as he walks back toward the bar. "I guess the highballs are on me."

A bear walks into a bar and orders a beer. The bartender says, "Sorry, we don't serve beer to bears in this bar."

"If you don't give me a beer, I'll eat that lady sitting at the end of the bar."

"Go ahead, see if I care. Rules are rules."

So the bear eats the lady and again asks for a beer. The bartender says, "Sorry, we don't serve beer to bears on drugs."

"What are you talking about?" the bear growls. "I'm not on drugs!"

"'Yes, you are. That was the barbituate."

"You can't be a real country unless you have a beer and an airline. . . . It helps if you have some kind of a football team or some nuclear weapons, but at the very least you need a beer."—Frank Zappa

"Without question, the greatest invention
in the history of mankind is beer.
Oh, I grant you that the wheel was also
a fine invention, but the wheel does not go
nearly as well with pizza."—Dave Barry

A drunk is sitting at the bar having a drink. He has a box resting on the bar in front of him. A guy asks him, "What do you have in there, pal?"

"A mongoose."

"What for?"

"Well, you know how I get carried away sometimes and drink too much. When I get drunk I see snakes, and I'm scared to death of snakes. That's why I got this mongoose, for protection."

"You idiot!" the other guy says. "Those are imaginary snakes."

"That's okay," whispers the drunk, showing his friend the empty interior of the box, "so is the mongoose."

Three mice are sitting at a bar in a pretty rough neighborhood late at night, trying to impress one another about how tough they are. The first mouse orders a Scotch, gulps it down, and slams the glass on the bar. He turns to the second mouse and says, "When I see a mousetrap, I lie on my back and set it off with my foot. When the bar comes down, I catch it in my teeth, bench press it twenty times to work up an appetite, and then make off with the cheese."

The second mouse orders two shots of bourbon, slams them down, and nearly breaks the glasses on the bar. He turns to the first mouse. "Yeah, well, when I see rat poison, I collect as much as I can, take it home, grind it into a powder, and add it to my coffee each morning so I can get a good buzz going for the rest of the day."

The third mouse lets out a long sigh and says to the first two, "I don't have time for this nonsense. I gotta go home and screw the cat."

A zebra walks into a bar. When everyone looks at him, he says, "Hey, don't worry. I'm over twenty-one."

A man walks into a bar and asks the bartender, "If I show you a really good trick, will you give me a free drink?" The bartender considers it, then agrees. The man reaches into his pocket and pulls out a tiny rat. He reaches into his other pocket and pulls out a tiny piano. The rat stretches, cracks his knuckles, and proceeds to play "Great Balls of Fire" by Jerry Lee Lewis.

After the man finishes his free drink, he asks the bartender, "If I show you an even better trick, will you give me free drinks for the rest of the evening?" The bartender agrees, wondering how any trick could possibly be better than the first. The man reaches into his pocket and pulls out a tiny rat. He reaches into his other pocket and pulls out a tiny piano. He then reaches into his jacket pocket and pulls out a small bullfrog. The rat stretches, cracks his knuckles, and starts to play "Bohemian Rhapsody," while the bullfrog sings along.

While the man is enjoying his free beverages, another bar patron offers him $100,000 for the bullfrog. "Sorry," the man replies, "he's not for sale." The stranger increases the offer to $250,000, cash up front. "No," he insists, "not for sale." The stranger goes to $500,000 cash, no questions asked. The man finally agrees and turns the frog over to the stranger in exchange for the money.

"Are you insane?" the bartender says. "That frog could have been worth millions to you, and you let him go for a mere $500,000!"

"Don't worry about it," the man whispers. "The frog was really nothing special. "You see, the rat's a ventriloquist."

"What contemptible scoundrel
has stolen the cork to my lunch?"
—W.C. Fields

A man walks into a bar and orders beer and a shot of whiskey. The bartender serves up the drinks, and the man downs the beer and pours the shot of whiskey into his shirt pocket. He orders another round, again drinking the beer and pouring the whiskey into his shirt. The bartender says, "Look, pal, I don't mind serving you, but my curiosity is getting to me. Why do you keep pouring the shots in your pocket?"

"It's none of your damn business!" the guy answers, "and if you give me a hard time, I'll kick your ass!"

With that, a mouse pops out of the man's shirt pocket and says, "And that goes for your fuckin' cat, too!"

HANGOVERS

What Are They?

Hangovers are a combination of dehydration (alcohol is a diuretic and tends to leach water from your body), shock (you've overdosed on booze), and malnutrition (many of the vitamins and nutrients that are normally housed in a healthy body are flushed as you expel the alcohol).

What Can Be Done About Them?

★ Drink moderately or not at all.

★ Drink plenty of water, both while drinking and after, which helps rehydrate your body.

★ Take aspirin (with a tall glass of water) before going to bed.

★ Rest.

★ Eat something to replace the nutrients you lost.

A man goes into a bar. As he sits down, a mouse jumps out of his pocket.

The bartender says, "Nice mouse."

The man says, "He's not any old ordinary mouse. He talks."

The bartender says, "Oh yeah, what about?"

"See that woman at the end of the bar? The mouse will tell me what color panties she has on."

"Yeah, right," the bartender says. "I gotta see this."

The man points to the woman, sets the mouse on the floor, and says, "Mouse, woman!" The mouse skitters over to look up at the woman's panties, comes back, and says, "pink." The woman smiles in agreement.

"Wow," the bartender says. "I gotta try that."

The bartender points to a woman sitting at the end of the bar and says, "Mouse, woman!" The mouse runs over, comes tearing back, and jumps up onto the bar and into the bartender's pocket, shaking like a leaf.

"What's wrong with you?" the bartender asks.

"I taught I taw a puddy tat!"

A mouse crawls from his hole at closing time, as the bartender is cleaning up. The bartender doesn't notice as the rodent finds a puddle of Scotch on the floor and starts lapping it up. Soon, the mouse jumps up on the bar and yells, "Now then . . . where's that frikkin' cat!?"

Done drinking, a cowboy walks out of a bar and a second later comes back in, mighty mad. "Okay," he growls. "Now which one of you hombres went outside and painted my horse bright red while I was a-drinkin?" Nobody answers, and the cowpoke draws his six-shooter and yells, "I SAID, which one of you mangy sidewinders painted my horse red?!

Slowly, one of the cowboys stands up from his seat. He is about six foot ten inches tall, and he pulls out what looks like a bazooka from his holster. "I done it," he growls.

The first cowboy holsters his gun and says, "Uhhh, I just wanted to let you know the first coat's dry."

Two guys walk into a bar. "I'll have a pint for me and a pint for my brother here, Jackass."

The two guys drink their pints, and the first guy says, "Okay, Jackass, your round. I'll have a pint of Guiness. I gotta take a leak."

As the first guy walks away, the bartender asks the second guy, "Why do you let your brother talk to you that way?"

Jackass replies, "I know. He aw . . . he aww . . . he awwwwww . . . he always calls me that."

A cowboy rides his horse to a saloon. The patrons watch as he lifts the horse's tail and kisses him on the butt before sitting down and asking for a drink. The bartender serves him and asks, "Why'd you just do that?"

"I have chapped lips."

"Does manure help them heal?"

"No, but it keeps me from licking them."

"Hey, bartender," says a customer, "What kind of bird is that?"

"Oh," says the bartender, "that's a Shredder Bird!"

"I never heard of a Shredder Bird," says the guy. "Can he talk? Can he do tricks?"

"Just watch," says the bartender. He takes a newspaper off the bar and throws it down on the floor. Then he turns to the bird and says, "Shredder Bird, the newspaper!" The bird swoops down from his perch and attacks the newspaper. Like a feathered piranha, he rips the paper until there's nothing left but tiny pieces of confetti.

"Wow," says the customer, "can I try?"

"Be my guest."

The man takes off his hat and puts it on the bar and says, "Shredder Bird, my hat!" The bird swoops down and picks up the hat with his beak and starts attacking. In no time, the hat is nothing more than a mass of shredded fabric and plastic. Then the bird flies back to his perch behind the bar.

Just then, a tough-looking guy walks into the bar. He yells, "Gimme a beer, *NOW*!"

Everyone is still startled by the bird's show, and the bartender is not moving fast enough for his liking. "How 'bout that damn drink? What the hell are you clowns looking at?" The tough guy soon sees the bird sitting on his perch. "What the hell kind of stupid-looking bird is that?" he asks.

"That's a Shredder Bird," says the bartender.

The tough guy laughs and yells, "Shredder Bird, my ass!"

A robber breaks into a bar and goes straight for the cash register. He's about to jimmy open the drawer and take the loot when he hears a voice in the darkness say, "God is watching." He turns around but doesn't see anyone, so he goes back to work with his crowbar. Again, he hears the voice: "God is watching." He turns towards the voice and this time sees a parrot cage in the corner. "Shit, it's only a parrot," he says. "Hey pretty bird, what's your name?"

"Moses," the parrot replies.

"That's a funny name. What asshole would name his parrot Moses?"

"The same asshole who names his Doberman 'God.'"

What's the difference between
a saloon and an elephant fart?
One's a barroom and the other
is a *BAROOOOM*!

Three pink elephants walk into a bar.
The bartender says,
"You guys are early. He's not here yet."

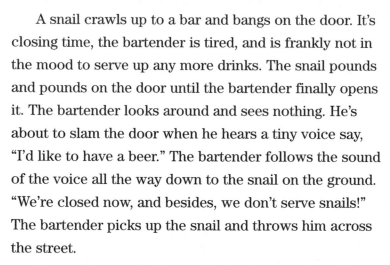

A snail crawls up to a bar and bangs on the door. It's closing time, the bartender is tired, and is frankly not in the mood to serve up any more drinks. The snail pounds and pounds on the door until the bartender finally opens it. The bartender looks around and sees nothing. He's about to slam the door when he hears a tiny voice say, "I'd like to have a beer." The bartender follows the sound of the voice all the way down to the snail on the ground. "We're closed now, and besides, we don't serve snails!" The bartender picks up the snail and throws him across the street.

A year later, as the bartender is about to close, he hears a pounding on the door. He opens the door, looks around, finally looks down, and there's the snail.

"*What the hell* was that about?!"

It's Christmas Eve, and a frenzied young man runs into a pet shop looking for an unusual Christmas gift for his wife. The shop owner suggests a parrot named Chet, who sings Christmas carols. "How do I get him to sing?" the young man asks excitedly. "Simply hold a lighted match directly under his feet," the shop owner replies. To demonstrate, the owner holds a lighted match to the bird's left foot. Chet begins to sing, "Jingle bells! Jingle bells! . . ." Then the man switches the match to Chet's right foot and the parrot begins to sing, "Silent night, holy night..."

The young man pays the pet shop owner and runs home with Chet under his arm. When his wife sees her unusual gift, she is overwhelmed. "How beautiful!" she exclaims. "Can he talk?" "No," her husband answers, "but he can sing. Let me show you." So the young man pulls out his lighter and places it under Chet's left foot, just as the shopkeeper had shown him, and Chet croons, "Jingle bells! Jingle bells!..." He moves the lighter to Chet's right foot and out comes, "Silent night, holy night..."

"What if we hold the lighter between his legs?" the young woman asks. Her husband shrugs. "Let's try it." So they hold the lighter between Chet's legs. Chet twists his face, clears his throat, and belts out, "Chet's nuts roasting on an open fire. . . ."

A guy comes walking into a bar with a turtle in his hand. One of the turtle's eyes is black and blue, one of his legs is bandaged, the other one's in a splint, and his shell looks like it was put back together with duct tape. The bartender asks the man, "What's wrong with your turtle?"

"Nothing," the man responds. "This turtle is very fast."

"C'mon! No turtle is fast," replies the bartender. "Especially not a beat-up one like that!"

"Okay, tell you what," says the man. "Let your dog stand at the end of the bar. Then go and stand at the other end of the room and call your dog. I'll bet you $500 that before your dog reaches you, my turtle will be there."

The bartender takes the bet. He goes to the other side of the bar and, on the count of three, calls his dog.

Suddenly the guy picks up his turtle and throws it across the room, where it narrowly misses the bartender and smashes into the wall.

"Told you it would get there before your dog."

"Two condoms walk into a bar…"

GAYS IN BARS

Two condoms walk past a gay bar.
One asks the other,
"You wanna get shit-faced?"

A bunch of guys are getting pretty soused at a bar and starting to feel their oats when the conversation turns to the question of who has the biggest penis.

Sick of hearing their boasts, the bartender says, "Why don't you just pull down your pants and lay all your penises out on the bar so we can prove who's biggest?"

So they all do it. Wouldn't you know it, in walks a gay guy.

"Can I get you a drink?" the bartender asks.

"No thanks, I'll just help myself to the buffet."

A guy walks into a gay bar.
Backwards.

A guy goes into a bar and orders five shooters.

Fearing the worst, the bartender asks him, "Geez guy, I'm sorry. Are you okay?"

"I just found out my brother is gay," he answers.

Same guy goes into the same bar a week later and orders ten shooters. The bartender again asks him, "Whoa, man, are you okay?"

"I just found out my other brother is gay."

The next week, the guy again goes into the bar and orders *fifteen* shooters.

The bartender asks, "Hey, doesn't anyone in your family like girls?"

"Yes. My wife."

How do you fit four gay guys on a barstool?

Turn it over.

How do you get them off?

Shake it.

A big, mean-looking biker dude ties up his nasty German shepherd in front of a bar, walks in, and orders a beer. Soon, a gay man swishes in and asks, "Who owns that sweet doggie tied up in front?"

The biker growls, "It's mine, who wants to know?"

"Well, I thought you'd like to know that Skippy is killing it."

"What the hell are you talking about?"

"Skippy is my French poodle."

The biker roars with laughter. "There is no fuckin' way your poodle can kill my shepherd!"

"*Au contraire.* Your dog is choking on him!"

Two oblivious cowboys walk into a gay bar. "I'm so thirsty I could lick the sweat off a cow's nuts!" one of them exclaims.

From the back of the bar, someone calls out, "Moo moo, buckaroo!"

A guy walks into a bar, but once inside, he realizes it's a gay bar. "What the hell," he says to himself, "I could really go for a beer right now." He sits down at the bar and orders a mug. The bartender asks him, "What's the name of your penis?"

"Look, I'm not into that. All I want is a drink."

"I'm sorry, but I can't serve you until you tell me the name of your penis. House rules."

Not knowing quite what to say, and dying for a beer, the guy looks at the man sitting to his left who is sipping on a white wine and asks, "Hey bud, what's the name of your penis?" With a smile and a wink, the guy answers, "Timex."

"Why Timex?"

"Cause it takes a lickin' and keeps on tickin'!"

A little shaken, the guy turns to the fellow on his right, who is sipping a strawberry daiquiri, and asks him, "So, what do you call *your* penis?"

"Ford, because quality is job 1." He adds, "Have you driven a Ford lately?"

The guy thinks for awhile, then tells the bartender, "The name of my penis is 'Secret.' Now how about that beer?"

"Why 'Secret'?"

"Because it's strong enough for a man but made for a woman!"

A belligerent drunk walks into a bar and hollers, "I can lick any man in the place!"

The nearest patron looks him up and down, then says, "Crude, but direct. I like your approach. Tell me, is this your first time in a gay bar?"

The world's greatest animal trainer is performing in a local tavern. "I will now put my head in the alligator's mouth," he says. He pulls down his pants and puts his penis into the alligator's mouth. He then pulls it out, unscathed.

"Now, ladies and gentlemen," he says, "I will give anyone in here $5,000 if you can repeat the trick.

In the back of the bar, an obviously gay guy announces, "I'll give it a try. But I'm not sure I can open my mouth as wide as the alligator did."

What do you call a gay bar with no place to sit?
A fruit stand.

Did you hear about the new lesbian bar?

They've got a pool table, but it doesn't have any balls.

A gay guy walks into a bar, approaches a group of drunk guys, and says "Anyone want to play fart football?"

"What the hell is fart football?" one of the guys asks. The gay replies, "Well, to score a touchdown you have to chug a beer, and for the extra point you bend over, pull down your pants, and fart."

Having run out of drinking games, one of the booze-hounds accepts this challenge and grabs a mug full. "Uhh uhh uhh, me first" says the gay. He proceeds to guzzle the beer. "That's six," he says. He then bends over, pulls down his pants, and farts emphatically. "Scoreboard says seven to nothing, me!"

The drunk laughs and downs his drink. He then bends over and pulls down his pants, trying anxiously to force out a fart. Suddenly, the gay guy jumps up, pokes his index finger into the guy's butt and yells, "Block that kick! Block that kick!"

A guy walks into a bar and orders a beer. He's enjoying his drink when he notices two beautiful blondes at the end of the bar. When he has emptied his mug, he says, "Hey bartender, another Bud, and give those ladies at the end of the bar a round."

"Here's your beer," the bartender says, "but don't bother getting them a drink. You're just wasting your time."

"Naaah. Give them each one on me."

So the bartender pours the girls fresh drinks. The ladies raise their glasses to acknowledge the gesture and take a drink. The guy figures he's in.

He strolls over to the girls and starts making small talk. One says, "Thanks very much for the drinks, but I have to tell you, you're just wasting your time."

"What the hell does that mean, I'm just wasting my time!?"

The other one says, "Well we're lesbians, we love to eat pussy!"

The man now has a huge smile on his face and yells to the bartender, "Hey bartender, make it three beers for us lesbians!!!"

How do you separate the men
from the boys in a gay bar?
With a crowbar!

Three men were sitting side by side at the bar,
sipping their drinks. "So what's going on in your life,
Bill?' one asks his friend. Bill replies, "I've got good
news. Dougie got a promotion. He worked his way
up from janitor at the bank and now he is an
executive. On top of that, there's someone special
in his life. He just bought his new love a brand new
Lexus."

The first guy says, "My son Jimmy also got a
promotion, and he's finally going to settle down. He
bought his fiancée a new house on the beach."

The third man seems a little upset at hearing this,
so the other two men ask him what the problem
might be. "I just found out that my son is gay. The
good part is his lover bought him a brand new Lexus
and a new house on the beach."

A man is enjoying a drink in a bar when he notices in a dark corner a gorilla in a cage.

"What's with the gorilla?" he asks the bartender.

"Observe." The bartender takes a whip and enters the cage. When he enters the cage, he pulls down his pants. He cracks the whip and the gorilla backs into the corner. He cracks the whip again and the gorilla approaches. The gorilla proceeds to give the bartender oral sex.

Once finished, the bartender leaves the cage and walks back to his place behind the bar.

"Wow, that was something," the guy says.

The bartender smiles. "Do you want to try it?"

"Okay," replies the customer. "But don't whip me too hard."

A straight man and a lesbian are arguing about sexuality. "My dildo can do anything a man can do," the lesbian boasts.

"Oh yeah?" says the guy. "Let's see your dildo buy you a drink."

Three desperately ill friends—an alcoholic, a chain smoker, and a homosexual—all share the same doctor. They go in for a checkup on the same day, and all, unfortunately, get bad news. The doctor tells all three: "You guys do everything to excess, and now I'm afraid you may have to pay the price. If any of you indulge in your vices one more time—there's no sugarcoating this—you are going to die."

The three shocked friends leave the office, determined to fight their temptations. While headed for the bus stop, they pass a bar. The alcoholic can't stop himself: "Can't I just go in one last time, for old time's sake?" he asks. He goes in, and the other two follow. Before his friends know what's happened, he throws back a shot of Jack Daniels. As he puts the empty shotglass back on the bar, he falls off the stool, stone dead. His shaken friends leave the bar.

As they continue down the sidewalk, they spy a half-smoked cigarette butt lying on the ground. "If you bend over to pick that up, we're both dead," the gay guy says.

SAFE BLOOD ALCOHOL
When to Say When

Body Weight	Drinks per hour			
	1	2	3	4
100 lbs.	.038	.075	.113	.150
120 lbs.	.031	.063	.094	.125
140 lbs.	.027	.054	.080	.107
160 lbs.	.023	.047	.070	.094
180 lbs.	.021	.042	.063	.083
200 lbs.	.019	.038	.056	.075
220 lbs.	.017	.034	.041	.068
240 lbs.	.016	.031	.047	.063

A blood alcohol content of .08% or more is evidence of intoxication (DWI, driving while intoxicated, is defined as having a BAC of .08 or more).

1 drink = 1 oz. of whiskey, 5 oz. wine, 1 can beer.

Rate of elimination: .015 per hour after drinking has stopped.

What are two words you don't want to hear
in a gay bar men's room? "Nice dick."

A guy walks into the bathroom of a bar and discovers two guys leaning over the urinal. One of the guys has got his pants down, and the other has got two fingers jammed up the first guy's butt.

"What the Hell is going on in here?" the new guy says. The guy using his fingers replies, "My buddy here has had too much to drink, so I'm trying to help him throw up."

"Sticking two fingers up his butt won't make him throw up!"

"Watch what happens when I put those fingers down his throat!"

What happens when two gay guys
get into a fight in a gay bar?
They go outside and exchange blows.

"Work is the curse of the drinking classes."
—Oscar Wilde

A gay guy walks into a bar in the Deep South with a huge German shepherd following him in. When he walks up to the bar and asks for a Scotch and water, the bartender looks him over and replies, "We don't serve your kind in here."

"I'm pretty thirsty," the gay guy says, "and if I don't get a drink soon I'll sic my dog Killer on you."

"Listen, pal," snarls the bartender. "Get out of here or I'll throw you out. And I ain't scared none of your dog!"

"You've left me no choice," says the gay, reaching down to unsnap the leash. "Go, Killer, get him!"

Killer jumps up over the bar, slaps the bartender in the face, and pours his master a mug of beer.

Did you hear about the raid at the gay bar?

The cops didn't arrest anyone, but they got $150 for their night sticks.

Four gay guys walk into a gay bar and they soon discover a problem: There's only one stool left.

One guy says "Lets flip for it"

But another replies "No, lets flip it *over*."

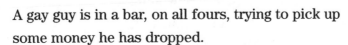

A gay guy is in a bar, on all fours, trying to pick up some money he has dropped.

The bouncer says, "Hey, you! Move it or I'll give you a foot up the ass!"

The gay guy replies, "I think you're bragging, but I'm game if you are!"

Favorite pick up line in a gay bar:
Can I push in your stool for you?

What do you call a fart
in the men's room of a gay bar?
A love call.

"Hi, I'm new in town.
Can I buy you a drink?"
"No thanks. I'm a lesbian."
"Oh, how are things in Beirut?"

"A leprechaun walks into a bar…"

ETHNIC
BAR JOKES

"But what hurt most, was the way she just looked at me and laughed."

A leprechaun walks into a bar and sees a sign that says, "Win a pot of gold if you can make the donkey laugh." As we all know, leprechauns love their pots o' gold, so he decides to go for it, and he does make the donkey laugh. He goes to the bartender to collect his winnings, and the bartender says, "Okay, but first you have to tell us how you did it."

"I can't tell you—it's a leprechaun secret."

"Then I'm not going to give you the pot of gold."

The leprechaun gets very angry and walks off. He comes back the next day and there's a new sign on the bar that says, "Win a pot of gold if you can make the donkey cry." So, anxious for the pot of gold, he makes the donkey cry, then again asks the bartender for the winnings. But the bartender repeats his demand: "First you have to tell me how you did it."

So the leprechaun says, "Oh, alright. Yesterday I told him I told him that I have a bigger penis than he does—and today I showed him."

Two guys are sitting at opposite ends of Kelly's bar late one night when one of them looks up and says to the other, "How's it goin'? You from around here?"

The other guy says, "Upper West Side."

"Me too. Where'd you go to school?"

"P.S. 66."

"Hey, so did I! What year did you graduate?"

"1980."

"Same year as me! What street did you live on?"

"Fourth Avenue."

"Holy shit, me too! What'd your dad do for a living?"

"He was a teacher."

"Unreal! Mine too!"

Just then another guy at the bar calls the bartender over and asks him, "What's goin' on?"

The bartender replies, "Not much . . . the O'Brien twins are drunk again!"

Where does an Irish family go on vacation?
A different bar.

One day, an Englishman, a Scotsman, and an Irishman walk into a pub and each order a pint of Guinness.

Just as they are about to take a swig, a fly lands in each of their pints, gets stuck in the thick head, and begins to drown.

The Englishman pushes his beer away in disgust. The Scotsman fishes the offending fly out, crushes it under his shoe, and continues to drink his beer as if nothing has happened.

The Irishman also picks the fly out, but he holds it out above the mug and starts yelling, "Begorrah! Spit it out! Spit it out, ya damned winged bastard!"

A Polish guy walks into a bar, holding out his hand filled with fresh dog crap, and exclaims, "Look what I almost stepped in!"

The traveling salesman walks into a bar and notices a sign that says: "Tonight Only—Luigi the Amazing Italian." He sees a table with three walnuts on it. Standing next to the table is an elderly Italian gentleman. Suddenly, the old man drops his pants, whips out his huge penis, and smashes all three walnuts, one after another. The gathered crowd erupts in applause and, once he pulls up his pants, they pat the elderly man on the back and buy him drinks.

Ten years later, the salesman's travels take him to the same neighborhood so he decides to stop in for a drink at the same pub. As he walks in, he sees the same sign on the door, although by now it's quite weathered. He can't believe the old guy is still alive, much less still doing his act! But there is the same table and the same, little Italian man, now ten years older. This time, instead of walnuts, three coconuts are on the table. The man drops his pants and smashes the coconuts with three swings of his amazing member. The crowd goes wild! The traveling salesman is astonished and hangs around after the show. "You're incredible!" he tells Luigi. "But I have to ask you—you're not getting any younger, why switch from walnuts to coconuts?"

"Well," says the Italian, "My eyes are notta so good anymore!"

A guy walks into a bar and sets a box down, opens it, and out pops a leprechaun. "I want a pint of beer and a shot of Irish whiskey for my little buddy here."

A man sitting at the end of the bar is amused by all of this. After the leprechaun drinks his shot of whiskey, the little fella runs up to the gawker and spits in the guy's face. Then he runs back to his friend's side.

The guy with the box says, "I'll have another beer and another shot for my friend."

After tossing back his shot, the leprechaun once again runs to the end of the bar and spits in the onlooker's face, then rushes back to his spot.

The guy with the box once again orders drinks, and the leprechaun proceeds to run down to the end of the bar. But this time the man quickly grabs the leprechaun and holds him in the air by his feet. "If you spit in my face again, I'm going to tear off your dick and beat you with it."

The leprechaun laughs and says, "Leprechauns don't have peckers."

"If you don't have peckers, then how do you pee?"

"By spitting."

132

Two rednecks are standing at a bar drinking their beers and talking quietly. A woman at a table behind them, who is eating a ham sandwich, begins to cough. After a minute or so it becomes apparent that she is choking, and the rednecks turn to see if they can help.

"Kin ya swaller?" asks one of the cowboys. No, signals the woman, desperately shaking her head. "Kin ya breathe?" asks the other. The woman, now beginning to turn blue, shakes her head again.

The first hillbilly runs over to her, grabs her by her ankles, lifts her up in the air, and yanks down her skirt and panties. He begins to slowly run his tongue up and down her ass. This shocks the woman into a violent spasm, which causes the obstruction to fly out of her mouth, and she begins to breathe freely again. The hick slowly walks back over to the bar and proudly takes a drink of his beer.

His pardner says, "Ya know, I'd heard of that there Hind Lick Maneuver, but I ain't never seen nobody do it."

Why can't Irish guys be lawyers?
They can't pass the bar.

Three men are drinking at a bar—a doctor, an attorney, and a redneck. While sipping his white wine, the doctor says, "For her birthday, I'm going to buy my wife a fur coat and a diamond ring. Then, if she doesn't like the fur coat she will still love me because she got a diamond ring."

As the attorney indulged in his martini he said, "For my wife's birthday, I'm going to buy her a designer dress and a gold bracelet. That way, if she doesn't like the dress she will still love me because she got the gold bracelet."

With that, the redneck throws back a shot of Jack Daniels and says, "I'm going to buy my wife a T-shirt and a vibrator. That way, if'n she don't like the T-shirt she can go fuck herself!"

The bartender is washing his glasses when an elderly Irishman comes in. With great difficulty, the Irishman hoists his bad leg around the barstool, pulls himself up painfully, and asks for a sip of Irish whiskey.

The Irishman then looks down the bar, squinting through the dark and smoky haze. He asks the bartender, "Hey, is that Jesus down there?"

The bartender nods, so the Irishman sends a shot of whiskey to Jesus, too.

The next patron to come in, very slowly, is an Italian with a hunched back. He shuffles up to the barstool and asks for a glass of Chianti. He also looks down the bar and asks, "Is that Jesus sitting at the end of the bar?"

The bartender nods, so the Italian says to give Him a glass of Chianti, too.

A Polish guy then swaggers into the bar and hollers, "Barkeep, line up a cold one for me! Whoa, is that God's Boy down there?" The barkeep nods, so the redneck tells him to give Jesus a cold beer, too.

Jesus soon gets up to leave. He walks over to the Irishman, touches his shoulder lightly, and says, "For your kindness, you are healed!" Feeling the strength come back to his leg, the Irishman dances a jig as he heads out the door. Jesus touches the Italian as he walks by and says, "For your kindness, you are healed!" The Italian feels his back straighten. He raises his hands above his head and backflips out the door.

Jesus walks toward the Polish man, but he jumps back and exclaims, "Don't touch me! I'm collecting disability!"

Father Murphy goes into a local bar and approaches the first man he sees. "Do you want to go to Heaven?" he asks, and the man says, "Indeed I do, Father." "Then for God's sake," commands the priest, "put down that drink and leave this pub right now." The man leaves.

The father then goes to the next man. "Do *you* want to go to Heaven, my son?" And the man answers, "Yes, Father, indeed I want to do that very thing."

"Then ye must get out of this pub at once!" bellows the priest. And the man does.

Much to the bartender's chagrin, Father Murphy continues this mission throughout the pub until he comes to the last man. "Do you want to go to Heaven, man?!" exhorts the priest. The man looks at his half-full beer, looks back at Father Murphy and says, "No I don't, Father." He then continues to sip.

"You mean to tell me, young man, that when you die, you don't want to go to Heaven?" asks the priest incredulously.

"Oh, well, when I die, yes Father, sure, I certainly do. I thought you were getting a bus trip together to go there right now!"

Three Englishmen are getting wasted in a pub when they spot an Irishman sitting off in the corner. For a little amusement, one of the Englishmen approaches him.

"Did y'know that St. Patrick was a sissy?" he asks.

"Oh, no, I dinnae know that," the Irishman replies. "Thank ye."

The man returns to his friends, complaining that he hadn't gotten a rise out of him. The second Englishman decides to try.

"Hey did y'know then that St. Patrick was a transvestite?" he asks.

"Oh, no, I dinnae know that. Thank ye for the info," the Irishman responds.

The second man returns to his friends, amazed that he, too, hasn't gotten to this guy. The third man thinks he has the solution.

"Did y'know that St. Patrick was an Englishman?"

"Oh, no. I hadn't heard that," said the Irishman. "But I believe that's what y'r friends have been trying to tell me."

An Irishman walks out of a bar.

Mr. Goldberg and Mr. Park are sitting at the bar. They are ignoring each other, absorbed in their drinks. Suddenly, Goldberg whacks Park on the side of the head.

"What the hell was that for?" the Korean asks.

"That was for Pearl Harbor!"

"Pearl Harbor?! That was the Japanese, not the Koreans!"

"Japanese, Korean—what's the difference?"

A little while and a few beers later, the Korean turns and whacks the Jew on the side of the head.

"Hey, why did you do that?"

"That was for sinking the *Titanic*."

"The *Titanic* sunk from an iceberg, ya schmuck!"

"Iceberg, Goldberg, what's the difference?"

An Englishman, an Irishman, and a Scotsman are sitting in a bar drinking and comparing their wives.

The Englishman says, "I tell you, my wife is so stupid. Last week she went to the supermarket and bought 300 pounds worth of meat because it was on sale, and we don't even have a proper refrigerator to keep it in."

The Scotsman says his wife is even thicker. "Just last week, my Sally went out and spent $17,000 on a new car," he laments, "and she doesn't even know how to drive!"

The Irishman nods knowingly. "Ah, I got one for ya. It kills me every time I think of it," he chuckles. "Me wife left to go on a trip to Greece. I watched her packin' her bag and she musta put a hundred condoms in there. And she doesn't even have a penis!"

What do you call twenty-eight rednecks in a bar?
A full set of teeth.

"My god! What happened to you?" the bartender asks Kelly as he hobbles into the bar on a crutch, his head bandaged, and one arm in a cast.

"I got into a little scuffle with Riley, I did."

"Riley? Why he's just a little guy," the barkeep says, surprised. "He must have had something in his hand."

"That he did," Kelly says. "A shovel, it was."

"Dear Lord. Didn't you have anything in your hand?"

"Aye, that I did. Mrs. Riley's left boob. And a beautiful thing it was, but not much use to me in a fight, I'm afraid."

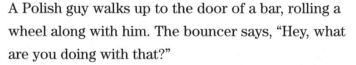

A Polish guy walks up to the door of a bar, rolling a wheel along with him. The bouncer says, "Hey, what are you doing with that?"

"Last time I came here, they said we had to have proper IDs and a tire."

An Irishman walks into a bar. The bartender says, "Hey, did you know you've got a steering wheel hanging on your pants?"

The Irishman says, "Yeah, I know. It's driving me nuts."

A Polish guy, an Italian, and an Irishman finish work and are deciding where to go for happy hour. The Irishman says, "Let's all go to O'Learys. With every third round, the bartender will give each of us a free Guiness."

The Italian says, "That's good, but if we go to Spignesi's, with every third round we get a free bottle of wine."

The Polish guy chimes in, "That sounds fine, but if we go to Kowalski's we drink for free all night and then go out into the parking lot and get laid."

"That sounds too good to be true!" the Irishman exclaims. "Have you actually been there?"

"Never been there myself—but my wife goes all the time!"

Goldberg meets his friend Weisman in a bar.

"Oy," Goldberg says as he sits down.

"I thought we agreed we weren't gonna talk about the kids," Weisman says.

A guy walks into a bar down in Alabama and orders a White Russian. Surprised, the bartender looks around and says, "You ain't from around here...where you from, boy?"

"I'm from Lansdale, Pennsylvania."

"Whatchu do up there in Pennsylvania?"

"I'm a taxidermist."

"What did you say, attacks-sea-derm-mist? What in hell is that?"

"I mount dead animals."

The bartender smiles and shouts to the whole bar, "It's okay boys, he's one of us!"

BARTENDING TERMS

Age Often used as a measure of quality. It is not always dependable, however, because ingredients are a factor.

Alcohol Common to all liquor. Spirits distilled from grain, grape, fruit, and cane are most common.

Ale Brewed from malt and hops. Usually stronger and slightly more bitter than beer. Color can vary from light to dark amber.

Aperitif A French term referring to a light alcoholic drink taken before a meal to stimulate appetite and enjoyment of the food and wine that follow.

Aromatized Wine This includes vermouth (Italian and French types), and the quinined or other aperitif wines of various countries, which contains 15 to 20 percent alcohol.

Beer Beverage brewed from malted barley and other grains cultured with yeast and flavored with hops. There are many varieties including ale, porter, malt liquor, bock, pilsner, and lager.

Bitters A very concentrated flavoring agent made from spices, roots, barks, herbs, and/or berries, usually used to provide a smoothness to biting whiskey.

Black and Tan A mixture combining equal parts of light and dark beer or ale.

Blended Whiskey Straight whiskey combined with neutral grain spirits.

Bock Beer German beer that is full-bodied, slightly sweet, and usually dark. Heavier, darker, richer, and sweeter than either lager beer or ale.

Bottled-in-Bond Whiskey Straight whiskey, usually bourbon or rye, produced under government control and supervision. Bonded whiskey must be at least four years old, bottled at 100 proof and produced in one distilling by the same distiller. It must be sorted and bottled at a bonding warehouse under government supervision.

Bouquet A wine's fragrance or aroma.

Bourbon American whiskey made using at least 51 percent corn grain mash combined with wheat, oats, rye, and barley.

Box Pour into and out of a shaker, usually only once. Gives the drink a quick mixing without shaking.

Brandy From the Dutch, meaning "burnt wine." A liquor distilled from wine and other fermented fruit juice (frequently grapes) and aged in oak casks and bottled.

Canadian Whiskey A blended whiskey, distilled from rye, corn, and barley. Produced only in Canada under government control. The Canadian whiskey sold in the U.S. is at least four years old.

Call Drink A drink made of liquor and a mixer, of which the liquor is a defined brand (e.g., Absolut).

Chaser A beverage drunk after another potable, to create a different taste.

Cobbler A tall drink of any liquor served in a Tom Collins-size glass with shaved or crushed ice and garnished with fruit and mint sprigs. Traditionally made with sherry, pineapple syrup, and fresh fruit garnishes.

Cocktail A beverage that combines an alcohol (usually brandy, whiskey, vodka, or gin) with a mixer (fruit juice, soft drink, or another liquor) and usually served chilled.

Cognac Superb brandy of France made only from grapes grown in the Cognac region.

Collins Any basic liquor combined with juice of lemon or lime, and served over ice cubes in a tall, frosted highball glass. Sugar and soda water are added, along with a lemon slice or cherry.

Cooler A tall drink made with different types of liquor, flavoring, cracked ice, carbonated beverages (e.g., ginger ale or soda water), and citrus fruit rinds.

Cordial A liqueur made by mixing or redistilling neutral spirits. Fruits, flowers, herbs, seeds, roots, plants, or juices—along with a sweetener—are added. Most cordials are sweet, colorful, and highly concentrated.

Corn Whiskey Whiskey made from a mash of at least 80 percent corn. May or may not be aged.

Crème A creamy cordial with a very high sugar content. They come in many flavors, including cacao and vanilla bean, black currant, mint, and violet.

Crusta A sour drink served in a glass that is completely lined with an orange or lemon peel cut in a continuous strip.

Cup A punch made up in quantities of cups or glasses.

Daisy An oversized drink of the sour type, normally made with rum or gin. It is served over crushed ice with a straw and sweetened with a fruit syrup.

Dessert Wines Fortified wines to which alcohol has been added during fermentation.

Distillation The process of separating the components in a liquid by heating it to the point of vaporization, then cooling it so it condenses in a purified form, thereby increasing the alcohol content.

Dry A term used to describe lack of sweetness in wine, liquor, or a cocktail.

Egg Nog A traditional holiday drink containing eggs beaten with cream or milk, sugar, and a liquor such as brandy, rum, or bourbon.

Falernum A syrup from the Caribbean made of mixed fruits, sugarcane, and spices, used as a sweetener for mixed drinks.

Fix A sour drink similar to the daisy, made with a large amount of crushed ice in a large goblet.

Fizz An effervescent drink made from liquor (traditionally gin), citrus juices, and sugar, shaken with ice and strained into small highball glasses. Soda water or any carbonated beverage, even champagne, may be used for the "fizz."

Flip An egg nog and fizz combination. Made with liquor, egg, sugar, shaved ice, shaken well, strained into short stemmed glasses for serving, and sprinkled with nutmeg.

Fortified Wine Includes sherry, port, Madeira, Marsala, etc.

Frappe An often fruity drink, usually combining several liqueurs and poured over shaved or crushed ice, or partially frozen.

Gin A spirit distilled from grain. Juniper berries and other botanicals give it its flavor. Most gin is colorless; however, some gins appear golden or straw-colored because of aging in barrels.

Grain Neutral Spirits Alcohol distilled from grain at 190 proof. Used for making gin, vodka, and other liquors, it is colorless and nearly tasteless.

Grenadine A nonalcoholic syrup flavoring for drinks, made from pomegranates or red currants.

Grog A rum-based beverage which also includes water, fruit juice, and sugar, commonly served in a large mug.

Hard Cider Juice of apples that is expressed and fermented.

Highballs Any liquor served in a medium to tall glass with ice, soda, plain water, ginger ale, or other carbonated liquids.

Irish Whiskey A blend that contains barley-malt whiskeys and grain whiskeys. The malt is dried in coal-fired kilns. The aroma of the fires does not influence the malt. Irish whiskey is heavier than Scotch, and is produced only in Ireland.

Jigger A small drinking glass–shaped container used to measure liquor. Also called a shot.

Juleps Made with Kentucky bourbon, sugar, and fresh mint leaves (muddled, crushed, or whole). May also be made with rye, brandy, gin, rum, or champagne. Served with shaved ice in an ice-frosted glass with a mint or fruit garnish and a straw.

Lace To pour onto the top of a drink. (Normally applies to the last ingredient in a recipe.)

Lager Beer that is stored in a cask or vat until free of sediment and crystal clear. A light, bubbly, and golden brew.

Liqueur A sweet alcoholic beverage made by infusing a spirit with a flavoring ingredient.

Liquor A distilled, alcoholic beverage made from a fermented mash of various ingredients.

Lowball A short drink made of spirits served with ice, water, or soda in a small glass.

Madeira A fortified aperitif.

Malt Liquor A beer that has a higher alcohol content than regular beer.

Maraschino Cherries Specially treated cherries, pitted and then macerated in flavored sugar. Popular as a garnish and as an ingredient in many drinks.

Marsala Fortified dessert wine.

Mash Grain or malt that is ground or crushed before being steeped. Used in brewing beer and in the fermentation of whiskey.

Mead Beverage made by fermenting honey, water, and yeast with flavorings such as herbs, spices, or flowers.

Mist A liquor (often an after-dinner liqueur) served over a glass full of crushed ice.

Muddle To mash or crush ingredients with a spoon or muddler (a rod with a flattened end).

Mull A sweetened and spiced liquor, wine, or beer served as a hot punch.

Neat A term referring to a drink served undiluted by ice, water, or mixers. (The opposite of "on the rocks.")

Negus A heated, punch-like combination of a wine such as port or sherry, spices, and sweeteners.

Nightcap An alcoholic drink taken before bedtime.

Nip A very small bottle.

On the Rocks A beverage served over ice cubes without adding water or other mixers.

Orgeat A nonalcoholic flavoring syrup prepared with almonds.

Pick-Me-Up A drink designed to relieve the effects of overindulgence in alcohol.

Port Full-bodied wine fortified with brandy and fermented.

Porter A heavy, dark-brown, strongly flavored beer. The dark color and strong flavor come from roasted malt. Porter is usually higher in alcohol than other beers.

Posset An old British drink from which eggnog was derived, consisting of heated ale or wine curdled with milk, eggs, and spices.

Potable Any beverage, particularly one containing alcohol.

Pousse-Café A drink made from several liqueurs and cordials, each having a different weight and color, so that when one is poured on top of another they layer and "float."

Proof The measure of the strength of alcohol. One (degree) proof equals one-half of one percent total alcohol. For example, 100 proof liquor is 50 percent alcohol.

Puff A traditional afternoon drink made of equal parts spirit and milk, topped with club soda and served over ice.

Punch A mixture of citrus juice with two or more liquors or wines, served cold, often in a large punch bowl.

Rickey A drink made with whiskey, gin, rum, or brandy combined with lime or lemon juice, cracked ice, soda, or any carbonated beverage, sometimes sweetened and served with the rind of lime or lemon.

Rum A spirit made by distilling the fermented juice of sugar cane, cane syrup, and molasses. It is bottled and sold at 80 proof. Aged in uncharred barrels, it picks up very little color. Caramel is added to create dark rums.

Rye Whiskey Distilled from a grain mash of 80 percent corn. It is usually aged in reused, charred oak barrels.

Sangaree A tall, sweet, old-fashioned (sans bitters) made with whiskey, gin, rum, or brandy, with port wine floated on top, or with wine, ale, porter, or stout, with a sprinkle of nutmeg garnish.

Schnapps In Europe, a generic term referring to distilled liquors.

Scotch Blended whiskey made from native barley grain and Scottish pot stills. All Scotch blends contain malt whiskey. The smoky flavor comes from drying malted barley over peat fires. Genuine Scotch is produced only in Scotland.

Shandy A beer cocktail originating in Great Britain, combining beer and ginger ale.

Sherry A wine fortified with brandy, added after fermentation.

Shooter A straight shot of whiskey or other spirit taken neat and often swallowed in one gulp.

Shot A small amount of alcohol. (A shot glass is the small glass in which such an amount is measured or served.)

Shrub A combination of spirits, fruit juices, and sugar aged in a sealed container such as a cask or crock, then bottled.

Simple Syrup Granulated sugar and hot water combined by heating, used as a mixer/sweetener for drinks.

Sling A beverage made like a Sangaree, with the addition of lemon juice and a twist of lemon peel. Served in an old-fashioned glass.

Smash A short julep made of liquor, sugar, and mint, served in a small glass.

Snifter A short-stemmed, pear-shaped glass used for serving aromatic spirits such as brandy.

Sour A short drink made by combining liquor with lemon or lime juice and a little sugar.

Spirits Alcoholic liquids distilled from fermented grapes, fruits, grains, potatoes, or sugarcane.

Stout A strong, dark beer. More redolent of hops than beer and made with dark-roasted barley, which gives it a deep, dark color.

Straight Up Term used to describe cocktails that are served up without ice.

Supercall Also known as top-shelf or super-premium. The high octane, often higher-proof alcohols, or super-aged or flavored versions.

Smash A small julep, served in an old-fashioned glass, made with muddled sugar; ice cubes; whiskey, gin, rum, or brandy; and soda. Garnished with sprigs of mint and fruit.

Sour A drink made of lemon juice, ice, sugar, and any basic liquor, similar to a highly concentrated punch. Garnished with a lemon slice and a cherry.

Straight Whiskey A whiskey that is distilled from grain but not blended with neutral grain spirits or any other whiskey, aged in a charred oak barrel for at least two years.

Sour Mash Whiskey A broad category of whiskey in which a portion of old mash is mixed with new to help advance the character and smoothness of the flavor.

Swizzle A tall, traditional rum-based cocktail filled with cracked ice.

Syllabub A beverage made from a mixture of sweetened milk or cream, wine, and spices.

Tequila Mexican spirit distilled from the fermented juice of the blue agave plant. Only tequila made near Tequila, Mexico, may bear the name; or otherwise it is called Mezcal.

Toddy A drink, served hot or cold, in which a lump or teaspoon of sugar is dissolved in a little hot water, combined with liquor, and stirred. Served with nutmeg, clove, cinnamon, or lemon peel in a tall glass.

Tot A small amount of liquor.

Triple Sec A cordial similar to Curaçao, but colorless and not as sweet.

Variety A term used to classify a type of grape used in the production of wine. A varietal wine uses only one grape variety.

Vermouth Herb-flavored wine fortified with brandy.

Virgin A nonalcoholic drink.

Vodka A refined and filtered liquor originally made in Russia from potatoes. In the U.S., it is often distilled from corn and wheat.

Well Drink A non-brand-name bar drink.

Whiskey Spirit distilled from a fermented mash of grains such as corn, rye, barley, or wheat, aged in oak barrels. After distillation, it is a water-colored liquid. During the aging period, it gradually attains its amber color, and its flavor and aroma. Whiskeys from various countries differ because of local grain characteristics, distillation techniques, and formulas.

Wine A drink made from the fermented juice of grapes. If another fruit is used, it appears on the label.

A Texan walks into a pub in Ireland and announces to the crowd: "Folks, your attention, please. I hear you Irish people can really put it away. I'll give five hundred American dollars to anybody in here who can drink ten pints of Guinness back to back."

The room is quiet. No one takes the Texan's challenge. One guy even walks out of the bar.

About an hour later, the same guy comes back in and taps the Texan on the shoulder. "Is yer bet still good, then?" he asks.

The Texan nods. The bartender lines up ten pints on the bar. Immediately, the Irishman chugs each one of them down, barely stopping to breathe.

The other patrons cheer, and the Texan nearly falls off his stool in amazement. He opens his wallet and counts out five crisp hundreds. "If ya don't mind me askin', where did you go for that thirty minutes you were gone?" the Texan asks.

"I wanted to bet you, but I had to go over to Murphy's Pub to see if I could do it first."

John O'Reilly hoists his beer and says to those assembled in the bar, "Here's to spending the rest of me life between the legs of me wife!" That wins him the top prize for the best toast of the night! He goes home to tell his wife.

"Mary, I won the prize for the best toast of the night."

She says, "Aye, what was your toast?"

John says, "Here's to spending the rest of me life sitting in church beside me wife."

"Oh, that is very nice indeed, John!" Mary says.

The next day, Mary runs into one of John's drinking buddies on the street corner. The man chuckles and says, "John won the prize the other night, with a toast about you, Mary."

She says, "Aye, I was a bit surprised meself! You know, he's only been there twice! Once he fell asleep, and the other time I had to pull him by the ears to make him come."

What has 72 arms, 36 heads, and an I.Q. of 12?
A redneck bar on Friday night.

A Scotsman is sitting in a bar in Cuba, just minding his business and swigging a beer, when a man with a large black beard walks in and orders a shot of whiskey. The bartender serves him, the man drinks it, and then he starts walking toward the door. The bartender says, "Hey, aren't you going to pay for that?" The man says, "Excuse me, Castro's Army." The bartender says, "Alright then," and the man leaves.

A few minutes later, another man with a large black beard walks in. He orders a drink and the same thing happens: The guy says "Castro's Army" and leaves without paying.

Watching this, the Scotsman gets an idea. He elbows up to the bar, orders a whiskey, drinks it, and heads for the door. The bartender yells, "Hey, aren't you going to pay for that?" The Scotsman answers, "Excuse me, Castro's Army." The bartender says, "Hey, where is your big black beard?" Thinking quickly, he lifts his kilt and says, "Secret Service!"

A guy is sitting at a bar having a few drinks, when he suddenly hears the call of nature. He goes into the bathroom and sees this really short guy taking a piss. He takes a spot next to him, and while peeing, he happens to look over at the little guy and sees that he's got a huge penis. He just can't help saying, "Man that is a big dick! I wish that I had a dick that big!"

"Well," says the little guy, "I'm a leprechaun and I can grant you one wish, and all you have to do is suck on me wang!"

In horror, the man exclaims, "No way, man—not even for a dick that size!"

"Fine, then," says the leprechaun, as he loads his weapon back into his pants.

After a minute of thinking, the man says, "Alright, I always wanted a big one. I'll do it." So the man starts to give the leprechaun oral sex. When he is finished, he says, "I can't believe I'm going to have a dick that big!"

And the little guy says, "And I can't believe you actually thought I was a leprechaun!"

MIXING MEASUREMENTS

Standard Units

Dash (one drop)	1/32 oz.	Half pint (U.S.)	8 oz.
Teaspoon	1/8 oz.	Tenth	12.8 oz.
Tablespoon	3/8 oz.	Pint (U.S.)	16 oz.
Pony	1 oz.	Fifth	25.6 oz.
Shot	1 oz.	Quart	32 oz.
Splash	1/8 oz.	Imperial quart	38.4 oz.
Measure	9 oz.	Half gallon (U.S.)	64 oz.
Mickey	13 oz.	Gallon (U.S.)	128 oz.
Jigger	1 oz.	**Wine and Champagne**	
Wineglass	4 oz.	Split (1/4 btl)	6 oz.
Split	6 oz.	"Pint" (1/2 btl)	12 oz.
Cup	8 oz.	"Quart" (1 btl)	25 oz.
Miniature (nip)	2 oz.	Magnum (2 btls)	52 oz.

Two hillbillies are sitting in a bar.

Jimmy Lee: "Hey, you wanna play twenty questions?"

Billy Joe Bob: "Sure. Lemme thinka somethin'."

Jimmy Lee: "Got it?"

Billy Joe Bob: "Yeah, got it. Ask me."

Jimmy Lee: "Is it a thang?"

Billy Joe Bob: "Yeah."

Jimmy Lee: "Can you eat it?"

Billy Joe Bob: "Yeah."

Jimmy Lee: "Is it horse shit?"

Billy Joe Bob: "Yeah."

A Polish guy is trying to pick up chicks in a bar but is having no luck. He goes home dejected, and his brother tells him, "Stosh, put a potato down your pants and try again." So he does. He still can't attract the attention of a lady. He goes home alone and disgusted. "I did what you told me," he yells at his brother. "I put a potato in my pants."

"Hey, Stosh," his brother replies, "maybe next time you should try putting it down the *front* of your pants."

An Italian guy buys everyone in the bar a drink as he announces that his wife just gave birth to "a typical Italian baby boy weighing twenty-five pounds." Congratulations come from all around, and many exclamations of "Wow!"

Two weeks later, the guy returns to the bar. The bartender says, "Say, you're the father of the big baby. How much does he weigh now?"

The proud father answers, "Seventeen pounds."

"Why? What happened?" the concerned bartender asks. "He weighed twenty-five pounds two weeks ago."

The Italian takes a slow swig of his Scotch and proudly says, "We had his hair cut!"

A guy walks into Kowalski's and there's a little Nativity scene on the bar. The guy says, "That's nice . . . but how come the three wise men are wearing firemen's hats?"

Kowalski says, "Well, it says right there in the Bible: The three wise men came from a fire."

A guy is traveling across the prairies of America and stops at a roadhouse. He stands at the end of the bar quietly sipping his beer and blowing smoke rings. This goes on for a while until an angry Indian approaches him and says, "Now listen buddy, if you don't stop insulting my wife, I'll kick the crap out of you!"

Two rednecks meet in a bar.

"I hear you've been having some problems with your well water lately," Redneck No. 1 says.

"Yup, but we've been taking all the necessary precautions."

"Oh yeah, like what?"

"Well, first off, we boil and filter the water."

"Makes sense to me."

"Then we add some chemicals that the Board of Health gave us."

"Great."

"Then we drink beer."

"Give an Irishman lager for a month and he's a dead man. An Irishman's stomach is lined with copper, and the beer corrodes it. But whiskey polishes the copper and is the saving of him." —Mark Twain

A redneck goes into a bar and orders a drink from the waitress. A little while later, she comes back. "Anything else I can get you, handsome?"

"Well, ma'am, I sure could use a nice piece of ass."

The waitress's eyebrows go up, she nods, and she leads him into the back room where she makes mad monkey love to him. When they're finished, they get dressed and return to their places.

"Now, honey, is there anything else I can get for you?" she asks, smiling.

"Thank you kindly, ma'am, but I could still use that piece of ass. Mah drink is a gettin' mighty warm."

A cowpoke rides into town and stops at a saloon for a drink. Unfortunately, the locals have a habit of picking on strangers, so when he goes outside he finds his horse has been stolen. He goes back into the bar, pulls out a pistol, and starts shooting into the ceiling. "Which one of you sidewinders stole my hoss?"

No one answers.

"All right, I'm a'gonna have anotha' beer, and if'n my hoss ain't back outside by the time I finish, I'm a'gonna do what I done in Texas! And I don't like to have to do what I done in Texas!"

Some of the locals shift restlessly. The cowboy has another beer, walks outside—and his horse is back! He saddles up and starts to ride out of town. The bartender runs after him, yelling, "Say, pardner, before you go—what happened in Texas?"

"I had to walk home to the Ponderosa."

Two Irishmen named Shawn and Pat are the best of friends. During one particular night of drinking, the two agree that when one passes on, in tribute the other will spill the contents of a bottle of fine Irish whiskey over the grave of the fondly missed friend. As fate would have it, Shawn is the first to fall seriously ill. Pat comes to visit his friend one last time on his deathbed.

"Shawn," says Pat, "Can you hear me?"

Faintly, Shawn replies, "Yes, Paddy, I can."

"So would you be rememberin' our little pact, then?"

"Yes, I do, Paddy."

"So you remember that I'm to pour the contents of a fine, old bottle of whiskey over your grave? A bottle which we have been saving for going on 30 years now?"

"Yes Paddy, I do."

"It's a very old bottle now, you know."

"And what are you gettin' at, Pat?"

"Well, Shawn, when I pour the whiskey over your grave, would ya mind if I be filterin' it through me kidneys first?"

"A blonde walks into a bar…"

BLONDES IN BARS

"I'm curious, why did you toss a coin
just before you came over here
and asked us if we'd like a drink?"

A blond walks into a bar and says, "I'll have a Coors Lite." The bartender gives her one, she passes out, and all the guys in the bar drag her into the back and have their way with her. The next night, she walks in and orders a Coors Lite. She passes out, and all the guys in the bar drag her into the back and have their way with her. The next night, she walks in and says, "I'll have a Miller Lite."

The bartender looks up and asks, "Why aren't you ordering a Coors Lite this time?"

"It makes my pussy sore."

A blonde sitting with her girlfriend at a bar says that she has given up men for life. "They lie, they cheat—basically they're just no good. From now on, when I want sex, I'll just turn to my vibrator."

"But what if the batteries run out? What will you do?"

"The same thing I do with my boyfriend: I'll fake an orgasm."

Three blondes decide to go out and celebrate. They walk into a bar chanting, "sixty-one days, sixty-one days..."

"Why are you chanting 'sixty-one days?'" the curious bartender asks.

"Because the jigsaw puzzle box said 'two to four years,' and it only took us sixty-one days!"

A blonde and a brunette are sitting at a bar watching the six o'clock news, and they see a report of a man about to jump from the George Washington Bridge. They continue drinking and talking, and hours pass. They soon find themselves watching the ten o'clock news. The brunette says to the blonde, "I'll bet you twenty dollars that the man jumps." Thinking for a moment, the blonde takes the bet. Sure enough, he jumps.

As the blonde reaches into her purse to pay the bet, she says, "My god, I just saw that same man on the six o'clock news. I didn't think he would actually jump again."

A blind man walks into a bar, taps a guy on the shoulder, and says, "Hey, wanna hear a blonde joke?"

The guy replies, "Look buddy, I think I should clue you in. I have blond hair. The man behind me is a 400-pound professional wrestler and he is blond. The bouncer is blond. The man sitting over to your left is also blond. Still wanna tell that blond joke?"

The blind man is silent for a moment and then says, "Nah, I wouldn't want to have to explain it five times."

Q: What is the mating call of a blonde?
A: "I'm soooo drunk."

And in the spirit of "equal time":
Q: What is the mating call of a brunette?
A: Has that blonde gone yet?

A beautiful blonde walks into a bar. A guy walks up to her and says, "Hcy, those jeans are pretty tight. How do you get into those?"

"You can start by buying me a drink!"

A blonde walks into a bar and says," Barkeep, gimme a martooni." The bartender goes back and fixes her a martini. She downs it quickly and says, "Barkeep, gimme another martooni." So he goes back and fixes her another drink. She downs that, then just sits there. After about ten minutes the bartender says," Would you like another?"

"No thanks," she says, "I got this terrible heartburn."

The bartender says, "Okay, I can't just stand by and let this happen. There are three things wrong here. Number 1: It's martini, not martooni. Number 2: It's bartender, not barkeep. And number 3: You don't have heartburn, your left boob's in the ashtray."

Why did the blonde run out of the bar and come back with a ladder?

Because she heard that drinks were on the house.

A brunette walks into a bar and says, "Gimme an M.L."

The bartender asks, "What's an M.L?"

"A Miller Light."

A redhead walks in and says, "I'll have a B.L."

The bartender asks, "What's a B.L.?"

"Bud Light."

A blonde walks in and says, "Can I have a fifteen?"

The bartender asks, "So what's a fifteen?"

"Seven & Seven! Duh!"

What do blondes and beer bottles have in common?

They're both empty from the neck up!

A lawyer and a drunk blonde are sitting next to each other at the bar. The lawyer leans over and asks the lady if she would like to play a fun game. The blonde just wants to have a drink, but the lawyer persists. "I ask you a question, and if you don't know the answer, you pay me five dollars, and vice-versa," he explains.

Again, she says no.

The lawyer, now somewhat agitated, says, "Okay, if you don't know the answer, you pay me five dollars, and if I don't know the answer, I'll pay you fifty dollars." This catches the blonde's attention, and she agrees to the game.

The lawyer asks the first question: "What's the distance from the earth to the moon?"

The blonde doesn't say a word, reaches into her purse, pulls out a five-dollar bill, and hands it to the lawyer.

Now, it's the blonde's turn. She asks the lawyer, "What goes up a hill with three legs and comes down with four?"

The lawyer is puzzled.

He takes out his laptop computer and searches all his references. He taps into the digital cellphone via infrared wireless connection and searches the Internet and the Library of Congress. He checks his Palm Pilot. All to no avail. After an hour, he hands her fifty dollars. The blonde politely takes the money and turns away to continue drinking.

"Well, so what *is* the answer?" the lawyer asks.

Without a word, the blonde reaches into her purse, hands the lawyer five dollars, and goes back to her beer.

"Bartender, I think this mug is broken," the young woman complains. "Every time I pick it up to take a drink, it hurts my finger."

The bartender takes the mug, looks at it, shrugs his shoulders, and pours the woman a beer from another mug.

"Ouch!" she squeals as she takes a sip.

The bartender looks at her curiously. "You're a natural blonde, aren't you?"

"Yeah, I am. What does that have to do with anything?"

"The mug isn't broken; you have a paper cut on your finger."

Did you hear about the blonde who wanted to open a new bar? When her lawyer explained to her that she needed a liquor license, she said, "Ewww, it's not gonna be *that* kind of a bar. That's disgusting!"

Four blondes go to the bar in their pickup. Three sit in the cab, and one sits in the bed of the truck. The three are in the bar for about an hour before the fourth finally comes in, looking frustrated and a bit sweaty.

"What took you so long?" they ask.

"I had trouble getting the tailgate open. I didn't want to break a nail!"

What does a blonde say when she sees a banana peel on the floor?

"Here we go again."

Blonde in bar: "Have you heard my knock-knock joke?"

Brunette in bar: "No."

Blonde in bar: "Okay. You start."

A young ventriloquist is on a nightclub tour, and one night he finds himself doing a show in a small bar. With his dummy on his knee, he's going through his usual dumb-blonde jokes when a blonde woman in the fourth row stands on her chair and starts shouting: "I've heard enough of your stupid blonde jokes. What makes you think you can stereotype women that way? What does the color of a person's hair have to do with her worth as a human being? It's guys like you who keep women like me from being respected at work and in the community and from reaching our full potential, because you and your kind continue to perpetuate discrimination against not only blondes, but women in general . . . and all in the name of humor!"

The ventriloquist is embarrassed and begins to apologize, when the blonde yells, "You stay out of this, mister! I'm talking to that little creep on your knee!"

What do you say to a blonde who won't give in?
"Have another beer."

Q: What did the blonde customer say to the buxom barmaid?

A: "'Suzy' . . . that's cute. What did you name the other one?"

A blonde is sitting at the bar crying her eyes out. The bartender comes over, hands her a box of tissues, and asks sympathetically, "Stacey, what's the matter?"

Between sobs, the blonde says, "Early this morning I got a phone call saying that my mother had passed away."

"Oh, I'm so sorry. Can I get you anything? Do you want to watch some TV, to lie down and relax on the sofa in the office?"

"Thanks, I'd like that very much. I need to keep my mind off things and just chill out."

"Good. If you need anything, just let me know."

A few hours pass, and the bartender decides to check on the blonde. He goes in the back room and sees her hysterically crying! "What's wrong now? Are you gonna be all right?"

"I just got a call from my sister. She told me that *her* mom died too!"

"Can I get you anything?" the bartender asks the blonde.

"No, thanks. I'm not drinking. I'm the designated driver. I just learned I'm pregnant."

"Wow, good for you! Congratulations."

"Thanks. I hope it's mine."

It's a dark and stormy night. A blonde and a brunette are sitting at a bar. Every few minutes, when lightning strikes, the blonde jumps off her stool and runs outside, then runs back in. This goes on for about a half hour. Finally, the bartender asks the brunette, "What's up with your friend?"

"She sees the flashes and runs out to see who is taking her picture."

What do you call twenty-four blondes in a box?
A case of empties.

"I'd like to order a bar pizza," the blonde says.

"Shall I ask them to cut it into six or twelve slices," the barmaid asks.

"Six, please. I could never eat twelve pieces."

According to legend, there's a bar in New York with a magic mirror: If you look into it and tell the truth, it will grant you a wish. If you lie—poof!—it swallows you up and you are destined to live in another dimension, behind the mirror, for all eternity.

One night, a brunette, a redhead, and a blonde walk into this bar. After a few drinks, they head straight for the mirror they've heard so much about. The redhead goes first and says, "I think I'm the most beautiful of us three." Instantly, she is surrounded by piles of money. The brunette steps up to the mirror next and says, "I think I'm the smartest out of us three." Presto!— The keys to a brand new Hummer appear in her hand.

Finally, the blonde goes up to the mirror and says, "I think . . . . . . " Poof!

A young husband gives his beautiful blonde wife a new cellular phone for their first wedding anniversary. She loves the phone, and he shows her all its features.

The next day, the blonde goes out to the local bar-and-grill with her girlfriends for lunch. Her phone rings and it's her husband.

"Hi, hon," he says. "How do you like your new phone?"

"I just love it. It's so small and your voice is clear as a bell. There's one thing I don't understand, though."

"What's that, baby?"

"How did you know I was here at the bar?"

A blonde goes up to the barroom cigarette machine. She puts in some change and buys a pack of smokes. She puts in some more change and gets another pack. Suddenly she shrieks with glee!

Some fellow bar patrons gather round to see what all the commotion might be.

The blonde turns around and says to them, "Hey, get lost. I'm winning here!"

A blonde goes into a bar and sees that it's on fire. People are staggering around and coughing; others are frantically trying to crawl out the door. She goes back outside and calls 911.

"There's a fire at Steve's Bar!" she tells the dispatcher.

"How do you get there?" the voice on the phone asks.

"Duh, a big red truck!"

A blonde walks into a bar with her blouse half open, exposing one of her breasts. Alarmed, the bartender says, "Uh, ma'am, is everything okay?"

"Sure, what do you mean?"

"Umm, you seem to have come undone."

"Oh my goodness! I left my baby on the bus!"

Why did the blonde quit her job as a bar restroom attendant?

She couldn't figure out how to refill the hand dryer.

Blonde in bar: "Excuse me, what time is it?"

Guy in bar: "It's 11:25."

Blonde (with a confused look on her face): "That's funny. I've asked that question maybe twenty times today, and I get a different answer every time."

A blonde says to a bartender, "Excuse me, but each time I sip my drink, I get a shooting pain in my eye."

"Well maybe you should take the swizzle stick out of your glass."

A bartender spots a blonde down on her knees at the end of the bar.

"Can I help you with something?" he asks.

"I dropped my diamond ring and I'm looking for it."

"Did you drop it right around there?"

"No, I dropped it by the ladies room, but the light's better over here."

"Shakespeare walks into a bar…"

CELEBRITIES IN BARS

BEETHOVENS FIFTH

A guy walks into a bar in the Empire State Building. He orders a huge beer, chugs it, walks over to the window, and jumps out. Five minutes later, he walks back into the bar through the window, orders another huge beer, chugs it, walks over to the window, and jumps out again. Five minutes later, he reappears and repeats the whole thing.

At this point, another guy stops him and says, "Hey, how the hell did you do that!"

"It's just simple physics. When you chug the beer fast enough and the rest of your body is warm, the warm air rises. And if the relative humidity and altitude are right and you hold your breath, you become lighter than air. Add to that the wind current swirling around the building, and you just float in the air."

"Wow!" exclaims the second man. "That is so cool. I gotta try that!" So he orders a huge beer, chugs it, goes over to the window, steps out . . . and lands— SPLAT!—on the sidewalk below.

The bartender looks over at the first man and says, "You know something, Superman? You're an asshole when you're drunk."

Shakespeare walks into a bar and asks for a beer. "I can't serve you." says the bartender. "You're bard!"

The Lone Ranger comes to town on the hottest day of the summer. He stops outside a bar and tells Tonto to run in circles around his horse, Silver, and to wave his poncho to keep a nice breeze going for the horse. He then goes into the saloon and orders a drink.

A couple of minutes later, a mysterious man dressed in black swaggers into the bar and says, "You the Lone Ranger?"

"Yes, I am."

"Just wanted ya to know ya left your injun runnin'."

Charles Dickens: I'll have a martini.
Bartender: Olive or twist?

A drunk staggers out of a bar and careens right into two priests. He says, "Hey your Holinesses, I'm Jesus Christ."

One priest says, "No, my son, you're not."

The drunk says, "Look, I can prove it—follow me." He takes the two priests back into the bar. The bartender takes one look at the drunk and exclaims, "Jesus Christ, you're here again?"

Jesus Christ walks into a bar, slams three nails down onto the counter and says to the bartender, "Can you put me up for the night?"

A man walks into a bar and asks for a pint. As he takes his first sips, he notices Vincent Van Gogh over at the other side of the bar. "Wow, one of the world's greatest painters, right here in the bar with me!" he exclaims. "Can I buy you a beer, mate?"

"No thanks, I've got one 'ere!"

A man wearing a stovepipe hat, a waistcoat, and a phony beard sits down at a bar and orders a drink. As the bartender sets it down, he asks, "Going to a party?"

"Yeah, a costume party. We're all supposed to come dressed as our love life."

"But you look like Abe Lincoln."

"That's right. My last four scores were seven years ago."

Mike Tyson invented a beer.

It's called Nick-A-Lobe.

Rene Descartes goes into a bar and the bartender asks him if he'd like another drink.

"I think not," Descartes says. Then he disappears.

"They who drink beer will think beer."
—Washington Irving

James Bond walks into a bar and takes a seat next to an attractive woman. He orders his "shaken, not stirred" martini, then gives a quick glance at the woman and casually looks down at his watch. The woman asks, "Is your date running late?"

"No," he replies, "Q has given me this state-of-the-art watch and I was just testing it."

Intrigued, the woman asks, "What does it do, Mr. Bond?"

"Well you see, it uses alpha waves to telepathically talk to me."

"I see. And what's it telling you now?"

"It says you're not wearing any panties."

"Well, it must be malfunctioning, because I'm afraid I am in fact wearing underwear!"

Agent 007 taps his watch and says, "Bloody thing must be an hour fast!"

Robin Hood and his Merry Men are celebrating their recent triumphs in a local Sherwood Forest pub. They all become intoxicated, and soon Friar Tuck begins to sing, as is his wont. With every drink, the good friar gets louder and louder.

Robin, fearing that the evil Sheriff of Nottingham might hear the racket, drags the good friar deep into the woods. He hides him in a hollow log near the river, but the friar sings on. Soon the Sheriff of Nottingham's men arrive to break up the high jinks.

The moral of the story?

You can lead a drunk to water but you can't make him hoarse.

"One martini is alright, two is too many, three is not enough."—James Thurber

Santa Claus decides to vacation in Texas because it's warm and he has heard that the people are friendly there. As soon as he arrives in town, people begin to point and say, "Look! Isn't he someone famous?"

Santa thinks to himself, "I'll never get any rest if people start asking to sit on my lap and try to tell me what they want. I gotta disguise myself." So he buys a cowboy outfit, complete with snakeskin boots and a ten-gallon hat.

As soon as Santa goes out, people begin to point and say, "Look! It's that famous Christmas character!" Santa rushes around a corner to hide. "It's my beard!" he thinks. "They recognize me because of my long, white beard!"

So Santa runs into the nearest barbershop and has them shave off his trademark beard. "I *really* look like everybody else now!"

So he walks into a bar with a big smile on his face. Suddenly a man shouts "It's him! It's the Christmas guy!" Santa can't believe it. He's sure he's thought of everything. So Santa walks up to the man and says, "How did you recognize me?"

"You? I don't know you who you are—but isn't that Rudolph that just followed you in here?"

A PINT OF MISCELLANEOUS BAR JOKES

"You look like a lady with a story to tell."

A guy asks a bartender, "Do you sell condoms here?"

The bartender replies, "Sure do. See the display right here behind the bar?"

"How much do they cost?"

"They're different prices for the different styles. Pick out the one you want and I'll give you a price."

So the guy points at a hot pink one with black polka dots.

"Okay, that will be $1.15 plus tax," the bartender says.

"I don't need the *tacks*!" the guy says horrified. "It'll stay up all by itself!"

A guy walks into a bar and shouts, "All lawyers are assholes!"

He looks around, obviously hoping for a challenge. Finally a guy comes up to him, taps him on the shoulder, and says, "Take that back."

"Why? Are you a lawyer?"

"No, I'm an asshole."

Sam is walking into a bar just as his friend is leaving, carrying a case of beer under his arm. He calls out, "Hey Steve! What's with the case of beer?"

"I got it for my wife."

"Good trade!"

A man sees a friend at a table, drinking alone. He walks over and says, "Hey man, you look terrible. What's the problem?"

"My mother died in August, and she left me $25,000."

"Gee, that's tough."

"Then, in September, my father died, leaving me $90,000."

"Wow. Two parents gone in two months. I'm sorry. No wonder you're depressed."

"And last month, my aunt died and left me $15,000."

"Three close family members lost in three months? I'm so sorry to hear that."

"Then, this month . . . absolutely nothing!"

A man walks into a bar with his underwear on his head. He orders a drink and the bartender asks, "Why are you wearing underwear on your head?"

"It's a long-running family tradition. We always do this on Thursdays."

"Then I have some bad news for you—it's Wednesday."

"Wow, I must look really stupid!'"

Three buddies are talking at a bar. The first says: "I think my wife is having an affair with the electrician. The other day I came home and found wire cutters under our bed, and they weren't mine."

The second friend says: "I think my wife is having an affair with the plumber. The other day I found a wrench under the bed, and it wasn't mine."

The third friend says: "I think my wife is having an affair with a horse. No, I'm serious! The other day I came home and found a jockey under our bed!"

A little guy is standing at the urinal in a barroom bathroom. In walks a big dude who sidles up to the neighboring urinal, unzips his fly, and says in a baritone voice, "Wooh, that water's cold!" At this, the little guy glances over and sees that the big guy's massive penis has apparently touched the water at the bottom of the urinal. The little guy is startled at the sight, and asks the guy, "Hey, what's your name?"

"Ben Brown," the guy responds in his cavernous voice. Upon hearing this, the little guy faints.

The big guy zips up his prodigious member and attempts to revive the little guy with some water from the sink. When the little fella finally comes to, he looks up at the guy and asks him nervously, "What did you say your name was again?"

"Ben Brown," the big guy replies. "Why?"

"Oh, that's a relief! I thought you said 'bend down'!"

A couple has a baby without arms, legs, or even a torso. The boy is just a head! But they love him nonetheless. On his twenty-first birthday, the father, with tears in his eyes, says: "Son, I'm proud of you. You are a testament to the human spirit. Let's go out and celebrate your coming of age."

Dad wheels him into the local pub and orders him the biggest, strongest drink he can think of. With all the bar patrons looking on curiously and the bartender shaking his head in disbelief, the boy takes his first sip of booze, and . . . POP! A neck and torso pop out from below the head. The father is thrilled and begs his son to take another drink. The boy nervously sips again and . . . POP! POP! Two arms pops out of his new torso. With tears of joy, the father begs his son to drink more, practically pouring the liquid down his throat. By now the boy is getting tipsy, and with his new hands he reaches down, spills some of the drink, then guzzles the last of it. POP! POP! The boy's legs appear.

At this point, the bar is in chaos. The father is literally on his knees, thanking God. The bartender is calling the local news channel. There's so much noise and commotion that no one notices that the boy has gotten off his gurney and is standing up on his new legs. He looks like a baby deer taking his first tentative steps. He stumbles through the front door and into the street, where a truck hits him and kills him instantly.

Seeing this through the open front door, the bar falls silent. The father moans in grief. The bartender resumes cleaning his dirty glasses and whistles a tune. The father looks at the bartender in disbelief and asks, "How can you be so cold and callous after what just happened?"

The bartender answers, "Well, it's obvious to me that the boy should have quit while he was a head."

A string walks into a bar with a few friends and orders a beer. The bartender says, "I'm sorry, I can get drinks for your friends, but we don't serve strings here." The string walks away a little upset and sits down with his friends.

A few minutes later, he goes back to the bar and orders a beer. The bartender, looking a little exasperated, says, "Look, I'm sorry, but I told you we don't serve strings here." So the string goes back to his friends.

Then he gets an idea. He ties himself in loops and messes up his ends. He elbows back up to the bar and orders a beer.

The bartender squints at him suspiciously and says, "Hey, aren't you a string?"

"Nope, I'm a frayed knot," he replies.

"Hey, did you know that beer contains female hormones?"

"Get outta here! Is that true?"

"Figure it out: If you drink too much, you start talking crap, nagging everyone in sight, and your driving goes to hell."

A young man walks in and sits down at the bar. "What can I get you?" the bartender asks.

"I want six shots of Jack Daniels."

"Six shots! Are you celebrating something?"

"Yeah, my first blowjob."

"Well, in that case, let me give you a seventh on the house."

"Thanks, anyway. But if six shots don't get the taste out of my mouth, nothing will."

A man walks into an empty bar, sits down, and orders a drink.

"Hey, nice tie!" comes a voice out of nowhere. He looks up at the bartender to see if he said anything. Apparently not. Maybe he was hearing things.

"Hey! That hairstyle looks cool on you!" The man looks up, but again the bartender is engaged elsewhere.

"Hey! Nice suit!" The man then calls the bartender over and asks him what's going on.

"It's not me," he says, pointing down to the bowl on the bar. "It's the complimentary peanuts."

A new bar opens, and for the life of him, the owner can't think of a name. He comes up with an idea that's as good as any other. He unlocks the door and a few customers walk in. The owner says to one of them, "You're the third person to enter my bar, and I'm going to name it after you."

"Okay," she says, "my name is Jill."

The owner looks her over and says, "I like your legs so I'm going to name the bar 'Jill's Legs'"

The next day, a bum is sitting outside the bar and a cop asks him what he's doing. He answers, "Waiting for Jill's Legs to open so I can get a drink!"

A man walks into a bar and says, "Give me three shots, one for each of my faraway best friends and one for me."

Every day after that, the man goes into the bar and orders the same thing. One day he goes in and orders only two shots. The bartender feels bad and says, "What happened, did one of your friends pass away?"

"No," the man replies, "I stopped drinking."

On his way home, Doctor Griffin made it his regular habit to stop off at a bar for a hazelnut daiquiri. The bartender would always have the drink waiting at the same time every night.

One afternoon, as the bartender was preparing the doctor's order, he was dismayed to discover that he was out of hazelnut extract. Thinking quickly, he threw together a daiquiri made with pureed hickory nuts and set it on the bar. Griffin came in at his regular time, took one sip of the drink, and exclaimed, "Wait a minute! This isn't a hazelnut daiquiri!"

"No, I'm sorry," replied the bartender, "it's a hickory daiquiri, doc."

A regular at Bob's Bar came in one evening sporting a matched pair of swollen black eyes.

"Whoa, Sam!" said the bartender. "Who gave you those beauties?"

"Nobody gave them to me. I had to fight like crazy to get these."

An armless man walks into a bar. He orders a drink and asks the bartender, "Would you mind reaching into my pocket and getting the money from my wallet?" The bartender obliges him. "Hey, would you mind tipping the glass up to my mouth?" The bartender does this, and the man sips until he finishes his drink. "Hey," the man asks, "Would you mind taking a napkin and wiping the foam from my lips?" The bartender does so, and says, "It must be very difficult not to have arms and to have to ask someone to do everything for you."

"Yes, it is a bit embarrassing at times," he says. "By the way, where is your restroom?"

"The closest one is in the gas station three blocks down."

It's Pete's first day on the job as a bartender. As he serves a customer a Manhattan, a piece of parsley falls into the drink.

"What the hell is that?" the customer asks.

"It's your Manhattan. And there's Central Park."

A man walks into a bar. He sees a good-looking, smartly dressed woman perched on a bar stool. He walks up behind her and says, "Hi there, good looking. How's it going?"

She turns around, looks him straight in the eye, and says: "Listen, I'll screw anybody, anytime, anywhere. Your place, my place, it doesn't matter. I've been doing it ever since I got out of college. I just flat out love it."

"No kidding? I'm a lawyer, too! What firm are you with?"

A young woman named Suzy is sitting at the bar, talking with her girlfriends about what makes the perfect mate. "The man I marry," she says, "must be a shining light. He must be musical, tell jokes, sing, and stay home at night!"

Flo, the elderly barmaid, overhears this and says, "Honey, it sounds like you don't need a man. You need a TV!"

Young guy at bar: "Hey, bartender. Pour me a cold one."

Bartender: "Go away, kid. You wanna get me in trouble or something?"

Young guy at bar: "Maybe later. Right now I just wanna beer."

A man is sitting at a bar during happy hour, enjoying a cocktail, when a gorgeous young woman walks up to him and whispers in his ear: "I'll do anything—anything at all—that you want me to do, no matter how kinky, for $100. Let your imagination run wild. But there's one condition. You have to tell me what you want me to do in just three words.'"

The man considers her proposition for a moment. He then takes out his wallet and slowly counts out the money.

Then he looks deep into her eyes, pressing the money into her hand, and says, "Clean my garage."

A man walks into a bar and orders a pint. He takes a sip, then tosses the rest into the bartender's face. Before the bartender can compose himself, the man starts crying.

"I'm sorry," he sobs. "I'm so sorry. I keep doing that in every bar I go to. I can't tell you how embarrassing it is to have a compulsion like this."

Just short of being angry, the bartender feels sympathetic. "Maybe I can help you out," he says. "One of our regulars, Dr. Bender, is a psychoanalyst. I've recommended a lot of people to him, and he's really helped them with their problems."

The man writes down the number, thanks the bartender, and leaves.

Six months later, the same man walks back into the bar. "How's it going?" the bartender asks, as he serves up a beer.

"Everything's great. I've been seeing Dr. Bender twice a week," he says proudly. He takes a sip of the beer, then throws the rest of the mug in the bartender's face.

"Those doctor visits don't seem to be doing you any good," the bartender sputters as he wipes off his face.

"On the contrary," the man claimed, "he's done me a world of good."

"What are you talking about?" the bartender yells, obviously getting very aggravated. "You threw a drink in my face again!" the bartender exclaimed.

"Yeah," the man says, "but it doesn't embarrass me anymore."

A man walks into a bar and sees a sign over the bar:

Cheese sandwich, $2

Ham sandwich, $3

Hand job, $10

He checks his wallet, then approaches the gorgeous barmaid.

"So, are you the one who gives the hand jobs?" he asks.

"Sure" she says with a devilish smile.

"Well, go wash your hands and make me a cheese sandwich!"

A girl walks into a bar and orders a Manhattan with a plum in it.

The bartender says, "Sorry, ma'am, I think you mean a cherry."

She says, "No, I mean a plum."

"Look, lady," the bartender says, "I've been tending bar for twenty years, and you're the first person who's ever asked for a Manhattan with a plum. Where did you ever get that idea?"

"Well, about three years ago I lost my cherry, and I've been plumb crazy ever since!"

A lady is drinking in a bar. After she ties a few on, she boasts that she can pee higher than any man in the bar and is willing to bet anyone $100. Of course, the men all snicker and line up to take the lady's money. They march outside. The woman declares, "Ladies first!" and eyes the wall of the building. She hikes up her dress and undergarments, leans back on one leg, and pees on the siding about three feet off the ground. The men all laugh, and the first contender confidently drops his pants, pulls out his penis, and aims high, at which point the lady exclaims, "Uhh uhh, no hands!"

A woman walks into a bar and sits next to a little old man on a bar stool. "I couldn't help noticing how happy you look," she says to him. "What's your secret to a long, happy life?"

"I smoke three packs of cigarettes a day," he says. "I also drink a case of whiskey a week, eat fatty foods, and never exercise."

"That's amazing! How old are you?"

"Twenty-six."

John sidles up to the bar and says, "Pour me a double, Eddie. I just had a fight with the little woman."

"Oh yeah? How did this one end?"

"Let's just say, when it was over she came to me on her hands and knees."

"Whoa! Really? Now *that's* a switch! What did she say?"

"She said, 'Come out from under that bed, you gutless weasel!'"

A guy walks into a bar flashing a big grin. "What are you so happy about?" the bartender asks.

"Well, you know I live by the train tracks. So, on my way home last night, I noticed a young woman tied to the tracks—just like in those old movies! I cut her loose and took her back to my place. Anyway, to make a long story short, I scored big-time. We had sex all night, all over the house, every position imaginable. It was amazing."

"Fantastic! You lucky guy. Was she pretty?"

"I don't know . . . I never found the head."

A man walks into a bar
and asks for a beer.
"That'll be one cent,"
the bartender says as he serves him.

"One cent!"

"Yes."

Sensing something might be going on, the man glances over at the bar menu and asks, "Could I have the New York strip steak medium well, fries, and a pint of beer on tap?"

"Certainly, sir," replies the barman, "but that will cost you some real money."

"How much?"

"Four cents."

"Four cents! Are you kidding me? Where's the guy who owns this place?"

"Upstairs with my wife."

"What's he doing upstairs with your wife?"

"The same thing I'm doing to his business."

A guy walks in and sits down at a bar. His face is all bruised and bleeding, so the bartender asks, "Hey buddy, what in the world happened to you?" The guy says, "Oh, I got in a fight with my girlfriend and I called her a two-bit whore."

"Yeah?" asks the bartender. "What did she do?"

"She beat me with her bag of quarters!"

Adam is talking to his friend at the bar. "I don't know what to get my wife for her birthday—she has everything."

His friend Bill says, "I have an idea! Why don't you make up a certificate entitling her to sixty minutes of great sex, any way she wants it. She'll be thrilled." Adam decides to take his friend's advice.

The next day at the bar, Bill asks, "Well? Did you take my suggestion?"

"Yes, I did."

"Did she like it?"

"Oh, yes! She jumped up, thanked me, kissed me on the forehead, and ran out the door, yelling 'I'll be back in an hour!'"

A guy is in a bar with a bunch of his friends. After a while of shooting pool and drinking, he whispers something to them. Then he walks over to the bartender and asks for a shot of tequila. He throws back the shot and says: "I'd like to make a little bet with you. I'll bet you $1,000 that I can piss in a shot glass placed all the way across the room, fill it up, and not spill a drop." The bartender says, "I'll take that bet. You're on."

So the man walks to the other side of the room and places the shot glass down. He goes back to the bar and starts pissing. He doesn't even get a drop in. He pisses all over the place, on everyone and everything within range. After he's done, the bartender laughs and says, "You owe me $1,000." The man pays the money with a big smile on his face. The bartender asks, "You just blew $1,000. Why are you so happy?"

The man replies, "You see those five guys over there by the pool table? I bet them each $300 that I could piss all over your bar and you'd laugh about it."

A man walks into a bar and the bartender says, "What can I get you?" The man orders a whiskey, which he throws down in one gulp.

"That will be three dollars," says the bartender.

"Screw you!" says the man. "You offered to get me something. I thought you were paying for it."

"Get the hell out of here," says the bartender. "I don't need your crap."

A year later, the same man walks into the same bar and encounters the same bartender, who looks at him and says, "You're the asshole who conned a drink out of me, aren't you?"

"Excuse me, but I have no idea what you are talking about. I've never been to this bar before in my life!"

"Sorry. My mistake. You must have a double."

"Hey thanks, dude. Make it a whiskey."

SIGNS THAT YOU ARE TOO DRUNK

★ At AA meetings you begin, "Hi my name is . . . uh . . . "

★ George Bush starts to sound like a reasonable guy.

★ You don't recognize your wife unless seen through the bottom of a glass.

★ Even rednecks stop doing jokes about your drinking.

★ Every night you find your roommate's cat more and more attractive.

★ Every woman you see has an exact twin.

★ You have a hard time staying on the sidewalk—but, hey, when did they install moving sidewalks all over town?

★ Hey, five beers have just as much nutrition as a burger —screw dinner!

★ You keep asking your wife, "Where are the kids?" but you don't really have a wife. Or kids.

★ Mosquitoes and vampires catch a buzz after biting you.

★ I'm not drunk, you're just sober!

⇨

★ Senators Kennedy and Packwood shake their heads when they walk past you.

★ Hey, that Tammy Faye Baker is kind of a babe!

★ That damned pink elephant followed you home again.

★ Beer: It's not just for breakfast anymore.

★ The back of your head is bruised. (Damn that toilet seat!)

★ The parking lot seems to have moved while you were in the bar.

★ The shrubbery between your garage and the house is starting to wilt from overwatering.

★ The whole bar says hi when you come in.

★ Two hands and just one mouth—now *that's* a drinking problem.

★ The bar owner actually carved your name onto your bar stool.

★ You go to donate blood and they ask what proof it is.

★ "I'm not under the affluence of incohol."

★ "Yeah, I have a drinking problem: I don't have a drink in my hand at the moment."

★ You can focus better with one eye closed.

★ Your liquid cleaning supplies keep mysteriously disappearing.

★ You fall off the floor.

★ You had your Spuds McKenzie tattoo removed and replaced it with Red Dog.

★ You have a reserved parking space at the liquor store.

★ You lose arguments with inanimate objects.

★ You sincerely believe that alcohol should be declared the fifth food group.

★ You wake up in the bedroom, your underwear is in the bathroom, you fell asleep clothed.

★ You wake up with a traffic cone between your legs.

★ You're in a rut at work: You just can't get past Senator from Massachusetts.

★ Your doctor finds traces of blood in your alcohol stream.

★ Your idea of cutting back is less seltzer.

★ Your job is interfering with your drinking.

★ Your twin sons are named Barley and Hops.

★ You've fallen and you can't get up.

A guy goes into a bar, orders twelve shots, and starts drinking them as fast as he can. The bartender says, "Damn, why are you drinking so fast?"

"You would do the same thing if you had what I had."

"What do you have?"

"Seventy-five cents."

A man walks into a bar and says, "Give me a beer before problems start!" He drinks the beer, and says again, "Give me a beer before problems start!" The bartender looks confused. This goes on for a few more rounds, and after the fifth beer the bartender is totally confused "When are you going to pay for these beers?" he asks. The man answers, "Now the problems start!"

A little old lady decides she wants to join a biker club. She knocks on the door of the local club and a big, tattooed, bearded Hells Angel type answers the door.

"I want to join your club," she declares. The guy is amused and he lets her in. All the shady characters stare at her. They sit at a booth.

"Okay," he says. "First I gotta see if ya pass the test. You have a bike?"

The little old lady says, "Yeah, that's my Harley out there," and points through a window to a Harley with a sidecar parked at the curb.

"Do you smoke?"

"Yeah, I smoke four packs of cigarettes a day and a couple of cigars while I'm shooting pool."

"Well, have ya ever been picked up by the fuzz?"

"No, I've never been picked up by the fuzz . . . but I've been swung around by my nipples a few times."

A man walks into a bar on a slow night and sits down. After a few minutes, the bartender asks him if he wants a drink.

"No thanks. I don't drink. I tried it once, but I didn't like it."

"Well, can I get you a cigarette?"

"No thanks, I don't smoke. I tried it once, but I didn't like it."

"Well, would you like to join some of the other bar patrons in a game of pool?"

"No thanks. I don't like pool. I tried it once, but I didn't like it. As a matter of fact, I probably wouldn't be here at all if I wasn't waiting for my son."

"Your only son, I gather."

A man walks into a bar and orders a beer. He tells the bartender, "I know how you can double the amount of beer you sell every day."

"Really!" says the bartender, "How?

"Very simple. Try pouring full glasses."

A bartender notices a guy poking at his hand and putting it next to his ear. He asks him what he's doing.

"Oh, it's the newest technology—I have a phone built right into my hand." The man puts his hand next to the bartender's ear, and sure enough, the bartender hears a dial tone.

After a few drinks, the man goes into the bathroom and doesn't come back for half an hour. Concerned, the bartender goes in to check on him. When he walks in, he sees the man with his hands on the wall, standing with his legs apart and pants down. He has the end of a roll of paper towels shoved up his butt. Shocked, the bartender yells, "What the hell are you doing!"

The man groans and replies, "I'm waiting for a fax."

Two ladies are sitting at a bar. "I read that eighty percent of all men think the best way to end an argument is to make love," says one.

"Well that will certainly change the game of hockey."

A guy walks into a bar on a Saturday night and orders a beer. He gulps down about half of it, then pours the rest on his right hand. After he does this three more times, the curious bartender asks him what in the hell he's doing.

"I'm getting my date drunk."

A hippie saunters into a bar-and-grill and places an order. "I'd like a cheeseburger. Make sure it's not too well done, not too rare, but just in the groove." The barmaid is a little annoyed at this, but serves him the burger.

"Could I get a pint of light beer?" he asks a short time later. "Not too much foam, not too cold, but just in the groove." Now the barmaid is a little pissed.

Soon, he calls the barmaid over again. "Could I get some french fries? Not too golden, not too greasy, but just in the groove."

"Wait," she says. "I have another idea. Why don't you kiss my white ass? Not too much to the right, not too much to the left, but just in the groove."

The local bar is so sure that its bartender is the strongest man around that they have a standing $1,000 bet. The bartender squeezes a lemon until all the juice runs into a glass, and hands the lemon to a patron. If the patron can squeeze one more drop of juice out, he or she wins the money. Over time, many people have tried but nobody has done it.

One day, a scrawny little man wearing thick glasses and a polyester suit comes in. "I'd like to try the bet," he says in a squeaky voice. After the laughter has died down, the bartender grabs a lemon and squeezes away. He hands the wrinkled remains to the little man. The crowd's laughter turns to total silence as the man clenches his fist around the lemon and six drops fall into the glass. As the crowd cheers, the bartender pays the $1,000. "You won fair and square," the bartender says as he shakes the little guy's hand. "What do you do for a living? Are you a football player or weightlifter or something?"

"I work for the IRS."

A guy walks into a bar and asks for a bottle of forty-year-old Scotch. The bartender pours him a shot of whatever, figuring that the guy won't be able to tell the difference. The guy downs the Scotch and says: "Hey, wait a minute! That Scotch was only ten years old! I specifically asked for forty-year-old Scotch. And I'm not paying until I get a forty-year-old."

Amazed, the bartender reaches into a locked cabinet underneath the bar and pulls out a bottle of twenty-year-old Scotch and pours the man a shot. The guy drinks it and says, "What are you trying to pull? That was twenty-year-old Scotch. I wanted forty-year-old Scotch."

So the bartender goes into the back room and brings out a bottle of thirty-year old-Scotch and pours the guy a drink. By now a small crowd has gathered and is watching the man anxiously as he downs the latest drink. Once again, the guy shows his displeasure and repeats his original request for forty-year-old Scotch. The crowd quietly murmurs.

The bartender realizes he can hold off no longer. He disappears into the cellar and blows the dust off a bottle of prime forty-year-old Scotch. Soon, he returns with the bottle and pours a shot. The guy cautiously downs the Scotch and says, "Now *this* is forty-year old-Scotch!" The crowd applauds his discriminating palate.

An old drunk who has been watching the proceedings with interest raises a full shot glass of his own and says, "Here's to you. Take a swig of this." The connoisseur takes the glass and downs the drink in one swallow. Immediately, he chokes and spits onto the barroom floor. "My God!" he yells. "That tastes like piss!"

"Great guess," says the drunk. "Now . . . how old am I?"

A sexy lady walks up to a bar and motions the bartender over. She run her fingers through his hair and asks to speak to the manager. The bartender is a little taken aback by her advance, but says, "He isn't here. Is there anything I can help you with?"

By now, the lady is running her fingers down his face and into his mouth, letting him suck on her fingers. She says, "You're sure he isn't here?"

"Yes, I'm very sure."

"Well, I just wanted to tell him there's no toilet paper, soap, or towels in the ladies' bathroom."

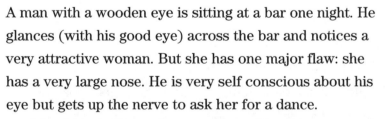

A man with a wooden eye is sitting at a bar one night. He glances (with his good eye) across the bar and notices a very attractive woman. But she has one major flaw: she has a very large nose. He is very self conscious about his eye but gets up the nerve to ask her for a dance.

"Would you like to dance with me?" he asks.

"Would I!" she replies.

The guy sneers and says, *"Big nose!"*

The Reverend John Fuzz is pastor of a small congregation in a country town. One day, he is walking down Main Street and notices a female member of his flock sitting in the town bar, drinking beer. He walks in and sits down next to her.

"Mrs. Fitzgerald," the reverend says sternly, "This is no place for you. Why don't you let me take you home?"

"Sure," she says with a drunken slur. As she gets up to leave, the reverend realizes that she has had too much to drink, and he grabs hold of her arm to steady her. As he does, they both lose their balance and tumble to the floor. After rolling around for a few seconds trying to rectify the situation, the reverend winds up on top of Mrs. Fitzgerald, with her skirt hiked up to her waist.

The bartender looks over the bar and says, "Hey buddy, we don't like that kind of thing in this bar."

"But you don't understand, I'm Pastor Fuzz."

"Well . . . I guess if you're that far into the game, you may as well finish!"

A very shy guy goes into a bar and sees a beautiful woman sitting at the bar. He gathers up his courage and asks her, "Um, would you mind if I chatted with you for a while?" She responds by yelling at the top of her lungs, "No, I won't sleep with you tonight . . . you pig!"

Everyone in the bar is now staring at them. The guy is hopelessly and completely embarrassed, and he slinks back to his table with a red face. After a few minutes, the woman walks over to him, smiles, and says, "I'm sorry if I embarrassed you. You see, I'm a graduate student in psychology, and I'm studying how people respond to embarrassing public situations." To which he responds, screaming at the top of his lungs, "What do you mean, $200 for a blow job?"

One day, Ed, known for always being broke and shabby, walks into his regular bar. Matt, another regular at the bar, says "Hey Ed, you're looking sharp. New wardrobe? And is that your Harley outside?"

With a big smile on his face, Ed explains: "I was walking to the grocery store when all of a sudden a girl rode up on this shiny new Harley. She got off her bike, threw off all of her clothes, and said, 'Take what you want.' So I did."

Three men walk into a bar and the bartender says, "If you can sit in my basement for a day, I'll give you free beer forever." So the first man says, "How hard can that be?" He goes down to the basement, but walks out after five minutes. "It's impossible," he says. "You've got a swarm of flies down there."

The second man also tries his luck, but can't take more than ten minutes.

Finally, the third man goes down and comes out a day later. The others ask him how he did it.

"It was easy," he says. "I took a dump in one corner and sat in the other!"

A guy walks into a bar and sees a golden mug on a shelf above the bartender. It says, "Win this . . . and free beer for LIFE!" He tells the bartender, "I'm game; how do I win this golden mug?"

"See that drunk guy over there? Knock him out in one punch. See that dog? He has a toothache, but no one can get the tooth out. Take the tooth out. See that old lady? She hasn't been screwed in a while, so . . . screw her."

The man walks over and knocks out the drunk. Then, he grabs the dog by the collar and brings him into the back alley. The bartender hears the dog yowling and making scratching noises, and then the man comes back in, buckling his belt. He pulls a pair of pliers from his pocket and says, "Where's the old lady with a toothache?"

A mechanic walks into a bar and orders a Michelob. As he begins sipping it, the bartender says, "You just had sex, didn't you?"

"Yeah, I did, about a half hour ago. How could you tell?"

"You've got a clean finger," the bartender says.

Three guys have had their fill and are getting ready to leave the bar, but the twisted bartender won't let them go unless they have twelve inches of dick among them. They soon realize he's serious, so the first guy whips his out and shows off his six inches. The second guy drops his pants and shows he's sporting five inches. Finally, the third guy shows his one-inch dick. The bartender says "Okay, that's twelve inches. You passed, you can go."

As they're walking out, the first guy says to the third, "Thank god you had a boner, or we'd still be there."

Three men are sitting at a bar discussing coincidences. The first man says, "My wife was reading A Tale of Two Cities and she gave birth to twins."

"Funny you should say that," the second man remarks. "My wife was reading *The Three Musketeers* and she gave birth to triplets."

With that, the third man jumps from his bar stool and shouts, "Good God, I have to rush home! When I left the house, my wife was reading *Ali Baba and the Forty Thieves*!"

A man has a few drinks in a bar and asks what his tab is.

"Twenty dollars plus tip."

"I'll bet you double or nothing that I can bite my eye." The bartender accepts the bet. The guy proceeds to pop out his glass eye and bite it.

He has a few more drinks and asks for his bill again. The bartender tells him that it comes to thirty dollars plus tip. He bets the bartender he can bite his other eye. Thinking he can't possibly lose, the bartender accepts the bet. The guy then proceeds to take out his false teeth and uses them to bite his other eye.

A cowboy walks into a bar and orders a beer. His hat is made of leaves; his shirt and vest are made of brown paper; and his chaps, pants, and even his boots are made of newspaper.

Later that night, he is arrested for rustling.

A man is sitting at a bar just staring into his drink. He stays like that for half an hour. Suddenly, a burly truck driver steps up to him, takes his drink, and downs it.

The poor guy starts crying. The truck driver says, "Come on, man, I was just joking. Here, I'll buy you a round. I can't stand to see a man cry."

"No, it's not that. This is the worst day of my life. First, I fall asleep and I'm late to work. I miss a meeting and my boss fires me. When I try to leave the building, I find out my car was stolen. I get a cab home and accidentally leave my wallet and credit cards in it. When I go inside my house, I find my wife in bed with the cable guy. I leave home and come here. And just when I am ready to put an end to it all, you show up and drink my poison."

A guy spots a pretty girl at the end of the bar. He approaches her and yells over the music, "Would you like to dance?"

"I really don't like this song," she answers. "And even if I did, I wouldn't dance with you."

"I guess you didn't hear me over all this noise. I said you look fat in those pants."

Three women are sitting at a bar, talking and drinking. They decide to give their husbands nicknames. The first woman says, "I would name my husband Mountain Dew, because when he mounts, he knows what to do."

The second woman says, "Well I would name Manny 7-Up, because he is seven inches long and always up."

The third woman says, "I would name my husband Jack Daniels."

"Girl you can't name your husband Jack Daniels," her friend says. "That's hard liquor."

"Exactly! That's my Jack."

While a bar patron savors a double martini, an attractive woman sits down next to him. The bartender serves her a white wine, and the man turns to her and says, "This is a special day. I'm celebrating."

"I'm celebrating, too," she replies, clinking glasses with him.

"What are you celebrating?"

"For years I've been trying to have a baby, and today my gynecologist told me I'm pregnant!"

"Congratulations! As it happens, I'm a chicken farmer and for years all my hens were infertile. But today they're finally fertile."

"How did it happen?"

"I switched cocks."

"What a coincidence. Me too!"

"You're not drunk if you can lie on the floor without holding on."—Dean Martin

STOCK YOUR BAR

Every well-equipped
bar should contain
the following:

Spirits

Gin
Vodka
Rum (light/dark)
Whiskey
    Bourbon
    Scotch
    Rye/Canadian
    Irish Cream
Wine
    White (dry)
    Red (dry)
Champagne
Vermouth (dry/sweet)
Tequila
Brandy/cognac
Beer

Fruit

Apples
Bananas
Cherries
Lemons
Limes
Oranges
Pineapples
Strawberries

Fruit Juice

Apple
Cranberry
Grapefruit
Lemon
Lime
Orange
Pineapple
Tomato

Mixers

Angostura bitters
Lemonade
Cola
Cream
Eggs
Ginger ale
Grenadine
Ice cream
Milk

Orange bitters
Sour mix
Sprite/7-Up
Tea/coffee
Water
   Soda
   Tonic

Garnishes, etc.

Cinnamon
Ice
Maraschino cherries
Nutmeg
Olives (black/green)
Salt/pepper
Sugar
Sugar syrup
Tabasco sauce
Worcestershire sauce

Liqueurs

Amaretto (almond)
Blue Curaçao (orange)
Chambord (raspberry)
Cointreau (orange)
Crème de banana (banana)
Crème de cacao (chocolate)
Crème de menthe (mint)
Frangelico (hazelnut)
Galliano (herb)
Godiva (chocolate)

Goldschlager (cinnamon)
Grand Marnier (orange)
Jägermeister (herb)
Kahlua (coffee)
Midori (melon)
Rumple Minze (peppermint)
Sambuca (anise)
Schnapps (various flavors)
Southern Comfort (peach)
Tia Maria (coffee)
Triple sec (orange)

Equipment

Bar spoon
Bar towels
Bottle opener
Bottle sealers
Can opener
Cocktail shaker
Corkscrew
Cutting board
Electric blender
Grater
Ice Bucket
Ice Tongs and scoops
Jigger
Juice Squeezer/extractor
Measuring cups
Mixing glass
Sharp knife
Strainer

One night a guy runs into a bar feeling as though his bowels are going to explode. He runs up the stairs to the bathroom, but can't remember which door it is. He opens one, looks around and sees a hole in the floor. Feeling desperate, he pulls down his trousers and releases his bowels. When he returns, everybody except the bartender is gone.

"Where'd everyone go?" he asks

The bartender replies, "Where were you when the shit hit the fan?"

It's New Year's Eve. A lady stands on her stool at the local pub and says that it's time to get ready for the celebration. "At the stroke of midnight," she says, "everyone stand next to the one person in the bar who makes your life worth living."

When the clock strikes twelve, the bartender is nearly crushed to death.

"Drink to me."—Pablo Picasso's last words

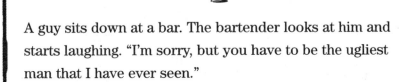

A guy sits down at a bar. The bartender looks at him and starts laughing. "I'm sorry, but you have to be the ugliest man that I have ever seen."

The guy says, "I'll have you know I can get any lady I want."

The bartender looks around and sees a hot, shapely blonde sitting at the table with her huge boyfriend, and tells the ugly man that he will bet him fifty dollars that he can't get the woman even to talk to him. The man agrees and says, "I'll bet you double or nothing that I can walk straight out the door with her." The bartender accepts. The ugly dude walks over, the girl jumps into his arms, and they walk toward the door, making sure to collect the hundred bucks on the way out.

The bartender walks over to the jilted boyfriend and says, "Damn that sucks! What happened?" The boyfriend replies, "I don't know. He just stood there licking his eyebrows."

A man is sitting at a bar having a cocktail, eyeing a gorgeous blonde on the next bar stool. She's checking him out, too. She looks over at him and smiles. Suddenly she sneezes, and her glass eye goes flying out of its socket toward the man. With his quick reflexes, he catches it in midair.

"Oh my god, I am sooooo sorry," the woman says as she pops her eye back in the socket. "I am sooooo embarrassed. Let me buy you a drink to make it up to you." They enjoy a few rounds together, and the woman invites him back to her place for a nightcap. They go back to her apartment, and after a bit of small talk, she leads him into the bedroom and begins undressing him. They have wild sex many times during the night, in every corner of the apartment. The next morning when he wakes up, she has already brought him breakfast in bed.

The guy is amazed. "You know, you are the perfect woman. Are you this nice to every guy you meet?"

"No," she replies. "You just happened to catch my eye."

A guy walks into a bar wearing a very attractive shirt. The bartender asks him, "Where'd you get the great shirt?" The man replies, "Tommy Hilfiger."

A second guy walks into the bar with really sharp pants on, and the bartender asks, "Where'd you get the great pants?" The man replies, "Tommy Hilfiger."

Soon, a third guy walks into the bar wearing really great shoes and socks. The bartender asks, "Hey, where'd you get those shoes and socks?" The man replies "Tommy Hilfiger."

Finally, a fourth guy, this one naked and out of breath, runs in, and the bartender says, "Look, buddy, we have a dress code in here. Who do you think you are?"

"I'm Tommy Hilfiger!"

An elderly couple walk into a bar and the husband immediately starts flirting with some young women. The bartender says to the wife, "Selma, doesn't it bother you that Leo is always making passes at the young ladies?"

"No, not really. I mean dogs chase cars, but that doesn't mean they know how to drive."

"Candy is dandy, but liquor is quicker."
—Ogden Nash

A sailor meets a pirate in a bar. The pirate is sporting a peg leg, a hook for a hand, and an eye patch. "How'd you get the peg leg," the sailor asks.

"Argh, matey. I got washed overboard one night during a fierce storm. No sooner did I hit the water than the damned white whale Moby Dick came and bit off me leg."

"How did you get the hook?"

"We were attacking one of her majesty's ships, and one of them scurvy dogs cut off me hand with his cutlass."

"Well then, how'd you get the eye patch?" the sailor asks.

"One of them flying devils, a damned seagull, shit in me eye," the pirate replies.

"You telling me you lost an eye from seagull shit!"

"Well, it was the first day with me new hook."

A guy walks into a bar and grabs a seat next to a woman reading *Cosmopolitan* magazine. "Hi, I couldn't help but notice what you were reading," he says, trying to strike up some small talk.

"It's really an interesting article. It says that, statistically, American Indians and Polish men are the best lovers. By the way, my name is Amy. What's yours?"

"Sitting Bull Zelinsky."

A couple is dining out when the wife notices a familiar face at the bar, downing Scotch after Scotch. "Michael," she says, pointing. "Do you see that man over there? That's Doug. He's been drinking like that for ten years, ever since I dumped him."

The husband replies, "Nonsense. Even that's not worth that much celebrating."

A guy is tending bar at a sophisticated New York club when two snooty women approach.

"So, where are you two from?" he asks.

"We are from . . . " one of them answers, "somewhere where people don't end their sentences with prepositions."

"Oh," says the bartender. "So, where are you two from, *bitch*?"

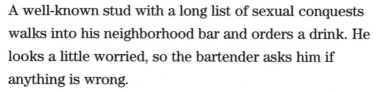

A well-known stud with a long list of sexual conquests walks into his neighborhood bar and orders a drink. He looks a little worried, so the bartender asks him if anything is wrong.

"I'm scared shitless," the stud replies. "Some pissed-off husband wrote to me and said he'd kill me if I didn't stop banging his wife."

"So stop banging!" the bartender says.

"I can't," the womanizer replies, taking a long swill. "The jerk didn't sign his name!"

"You can't drown yourself in drink. I've tried—you float."—John Barrymore

A guy walks into a bar and orders a beer. The bartender looks at him and says, "Have you seen Ilene?" The guy is understandably perplexed by this left-field question and asks, "Ilene who?" The bartender replies, "I lean over, and you kiss my ass."

The man is offended, and he storms out and goes to the bar across the street. While drinking there, he shares what the other bartender said to him. The new bartender tells him, "You know what you should do? You should go back over there and ask him if he has seen Ben. When he says 'Ben who?' you say, 'Bend over and kiss my ass."

So the guy goes back across the street and says, "Have you seen Ben?" The bartender replies, "Yep, Ben just went out the door with Ilene."

"Ilene who?"

A guy walks into a bar and asks for a rum and Coke. The bartender puts an apple on the table. The guy looks at the apple and repeats, "I said I want a rum and Coke."

"Just try the apple," the bartender replies. So the guy bites into the apple and says, "Wow, this tastes like rum."

"Turn it around, the bartender instructs. He bites in again and says, "Wow, it tastes like Coke."

A minute later another guy walks in and asks the bartender for a gin and tonic. The bartender puts an apple on the table. Much like the first guy, he repeats himself, thinking maybe the bartender has misheard him. The first guy urges him to try it. So the guy bites into the apple. "Wow, it tastes like gin!" he says. The bartender tells him to turn it around. He bites into it again. "Hey, it tastes like tonic."

Later on, another guy walks in and joins the first two guys. The guys are so excited about the apples they've been enjoying that they tell the newcomer that the bartender has an apple for every taste. So the third guy asks for an apple that tastes like pussy. The bartender puts the apple on the table, the guy bites into it. "This tastes like shit!" he yells.

The bartender replies, "Turn it around!"

"The problem with the world is that everyone is a few drinks behind."—Humphrey Bogart

The seventy-five-year-old man is summoned to his doctor's office. He's recently had a cancer biopsy and the doctor tells him he is terminal—he's going to die soon. The old man replies, "I've had a good life and raised a fine son to manhood. I'll just enjoy the remaining time I have." He calls his son and invites him to the local pub so he can break the news. The son takes it hard, but the old man reassures him that he will have a nice inheritance and that he should enjoy his own life.

The old man proceeds to tell everyone in the pub that he has full-blown AIDS. The son whispers to his father, "Dad I thought you had colon cancer."

"Yeah, I do, but I don't want these bastards banging your mother after I'm gone."

An elderly woman asks the bartender for a Scotch and two drops of water. As the bartender gives her the drink, she says, "It's my eightieth birthday today, and I'm here to celebrate."

"Well, God bless you! Since it's your birthday, I'll buy the drink."

Soon, everyone in the bar is buying the sweet old lady drinks, and each time she says, "Bartender, I want a Scotch and two drops of water."

Finally, he says, "Ma'am, I'm dying of curiosity. Why the strange recipe?"

"Sonny, you'll learn when you're my age that you can hold your liquor but you sure can't hold your water."

Mike and Tom are chatting at the bar. "I just got kicked off the course for breaking sixty," Mike says.

Tom looks at him, amazed. "Breaking sixty? That's amazing!"

Mike smiled and said, "Yeah! Who knew a golf cart could go that fast!"

A man goes into a bar and orders five shots. The bartender gives him an odd look, but he lines the shots up on the bar. The man downs them all quickly. As he finishes the last one, he calls out, "Four shots, please!" The bartender serves up four shots, and the man downs them all. He belches loudly and orders three. And one after the other, he knocks them back. "Two shots!" he slurs, swaying on the bench, and the bartender places two shots in front of him. As the guy slams down the last one, he says, "One shot, bartender." So the bartender fills the glass, and the man sits there, staring at it for a moment, trying to focus. Then he looks at the barman and says, "You know, it's a funny thing, but the less I drink, the drunker I get."

A woman walks into a bar that has a sign over the door, For Men Only.

"I'm sorry, ma'am," says the bartender. "We serve only men in this place."

"That's okay. I'll take two, please."

A guy walks through the door of a bar and slips on a pile of crap at the threshold. He scrapes his foot on the floor, walks up to the bar, and orders a drink. A few minutes later, another guy walks through the door, yelling and screaming as he slips and falls right into the pile of crap. He cleans himself off as best he can and sits down next to the other guy.

The first guy says, "I did that!" So the new guy punches him and leaves.

A guy runs into a bar and asks the bartender for a glass of water. Rather than serving him, the bartender pulls out a pistol and says, "Buddy, we don't serve water here."

"Thanks a lot," the guy says, and leaves.

A guy sitting nearby says to the bartender, "Why'd that guy just say thanks, when you flashed a gun at him and didn't serve him?"

"He had the hiccups."

A guy goes into the bar with a carrot in his ear. He orders a drink. The bartender is dying to mention the carrot but decides against it.

The next day, the same guy, still with the carrot, goes to the same bar. Again, the bartender wants to say something but doesn't.

The third day, the carrot guy goes to the same bar and orders a drink. The bartender can't stand it anymore. He says, "Hey, I just have to mention it: You've got a carrot in your ear!"

"What'd you say? I can't hear you! I've got a carrot in my ear."

A guy walks into a bar with a carrot in his ear. He sits down for a few drinks and the bartender ignores the carrot, not wanting to offend the guy. This goes on for four nights. On the fifth night, the guy walks in with a broccoli spear in his ear. "I've got to ask you, buddy— why do you have broccoli in your ear?"

"They were out of carrots."

Three vampires walk into a bar. The first one says, "I'll have a pint of blood."

The second one says, "I'll have one, too."

The third one says, "I think I'll have a pint of plasma."

The bartender says, "So, that'll be two Bloods and a Blood Lite?"

Two ladies go into a singles bar looking for a date. They spy a guy standing, and one walks over to strike up a conversation. "You look very pale," she observes. "I guess you don't get out in the sun too often."

"No, not really. I just got out of solitary confinement."

"Wow, prison! What were you in for? Fraud? Embezzlement?"

"I stabbed my wife to death. Then I dismembered her and fed her to my German shepherd."

The lady waves over to her friend. "Hey Kathy, c'mere! He's *single*!"

A woman stumbles into a bar, puts down a load of packages with a grunt, places her baby's seat on a bar stool, and flops down onto the stool next to it. "I am so exhausted," she says. "I just need to get a seltzer." After a few minutes, she feels the eyes of a man a few stools away staring at her and her baby. "What's your problem?" she asks.

"I'm sorry, ma'am, I couldn't help myself. It's just that I've never seen such an ugly baby in my life!"

"Why, you son of a bitch!" she yells, throwing her drink at the offending man. She's just about the throw the ashtray at him when the bartender grabs her hand.

"Calm down now, ma'am. Pay no attention to Terry. He's just had a few too many. I'm sure he doesn't mean anything by it. Now let me get you a fresh drink, and a nice ripe banana for your monkey."

Two friends meet in a bar. One orders a beer, the other orders a Sprite. "I gotta take it easy tonight," the soda drinker says. "Last night I did some things I'm a little ashamed of."

"Well, why'd you have to get drunk in the first place?" his friend asks.

"I didn't get drunk in the first place," he replies. "I got drunk in the fourth place."

A man walks into a bar visibly upset. "What up, pal?" the bartender asks. "You look pretty down in the mouth."

"Yeah, I am. I had everything any man could ever want: a gorgeous sex-crazed woman, a beautiful home on the beach, piles of money, a Hummer . . ."

"So what happened?"

"My wife walked in!"

A man walks into a bar, sits down, reaches into his coat pocket, and pulls out a beautiful, tiny woman. She has an hourglass figure, is dressed to kill, but is no more than a eight inches tall. She begins to dance a sexy dance on the bar. "Can I have a beer and a small gin and tonic for my friend Tiffany here?" the man asks the bartender.

The bartender fixes the drinks, serves them, and says, "I'm sure you already know this, "but she is gorgeous, and no bigger than your hand!"

"Yeah, I know," the guy says, 'but she's a lot better."

A guy walks into a bar and orders a whiskey sour. He's obviously feeling pretty good, whistling and smiling from ear to ear. "What are you so happy about?" the bartender asks. "Good news?"

"I'll say! For years, my wife's been bugging me for a Jaguar. I finally got her one, and the damn thing ate her."

A regular in a bar notices a woman who keeps coming in alone, night after night. After the second week, he decides to make his move. "No, thank you," the woman says politely. "This may sound rather odd in this day and age, but I'm keeping myself pure until I meet the man I love."

"That must be rather difficult," the man replies.

"Oh, I don't mind too much," she says. "But my husband is pretty pissed about it."

Max is sitting at the bar, obviously dejected. The bartender serves him and asks, "What's wrong, pal?"

"I'll never understand women," Max says. "The other night my wife threw me a birthday party. She told me that later on, as her gift to me, I could do with her whatever I wanted."

"Wow! That sounds like a great gift. So why are you so unhappy?"

"Well, I thought about it and sent her home to her mother. Now she won't even speak to me."

A man runs into a bar and nervously jumps onto a bar stool. "Give me a double shot of Johnny Walker Red on the rocks." Realizing the guy is shaken, the bartender serves him quickly and sits the bottle down on the bar next to him. The guy chugs down the shot, and the bartender pours another. After a few minutes, the guy takes a deep breath, composes himself, and asks, "How tall are penguins?"

The bartender holds his hand about ten inches over the bar.

The guy shakes his head and takes another shot. "How tall did you say penguins were?"

The bartender holds his hand out again, then asks, "Why, what's up?"

"Well, if penguins are only that tall, I think I ran over two nuns on the way in here!"

An old man is sitting at a bar. In walks a young man with a spiked mohawk haircut dyed all the colors of the rainbow. The old guy keeps staring at him. The young dude says, "What's the matter, Pops? Never done anything wild in your life?"

"You know, actually I got real drunk once and fucked a peacock. I was just thinking you might be my son."

After noticing a beautiful young redhead sitting on her own in a pub, a studly young man confidently strolls over to her table and says, "What can I get you, gorgeous?"

The woman blushes and replies, "If you're sure you don't mind, I'll have a large stiff one, please."

"Would that be before or after I get the drinks?"

After spending a happy evening drinking together, two acquaintances promise to meet again in ten years at the same bar, same time. Ten years later, the first guy walks in, looks around, and sure enough, there is his friend on the same bar stool. He clasps the old friend's hand and cries, "The day we left, I didn't think I'd really see you here again!"

The friend looks up, sways slightly, and asks, "Who left?"

A man walks into a bar and orders a beer. When the bartender asks him to pay up, the guy says, "Uh, I have no money, but I'll tell you what. For the beer, I will sing through my asshole."

The bartender is a little bit skeptical, but says, "Well, if you really can do that, I guess it's worth a beer." The guy gets up on a stool, drop his pants, bends over, then shits all over the bar. The bartender screams, "What the hell did you do that for?"

The guy replies, "Sorry, man, I was just clearing my throat."

A guy walks into a bar and orders a beer. He looks down the bar and sees a man sitting there with a shrunken head the size of a cue ball. Curious, he walks over. "Exuse me sir, I don't mean to be rude but I notice you have a small head. Is it a birth defect?"

Monsieur Tinyhead recounts his story. "No, it's not that at all. My shop was torpedoed by a German U-Boat in World War II. I was the only survivor and I swam to the shore of a deserted island. One day, while I was walking around the beach looking for food, I saw a brass lamp bobbing in the surf. I picked up the lamp, dried it off with my shirt, and—wouldn't you know it? A beautiful blonde genie appeared! She thanked me for freeing her from her prison, and to repay me she offered to grant me three wishes.

"I thought about it for about half a second. For my first wish, I wanted to return to the U.S. The genie waved her hand and POOF! I was back in my hometown. My second wish was to have all the money I would ever need. POOF! Wish granted. At that point I was feeling pretty good. In fact, I was rather horny since I had been on that island for three months. So I looked at the genie and said, 'How about a little head?'"

Two buddies are sharing drinks while discussing their wives. "Does your wife ever do it doggy style?" asked one of the guys.

"Not exactly," his friend replies. "She's more into being a trick dog."

"Oh, I see. Kinky stuff, huh?"

"Well, not exactly. Whenever I make a move, she rolls over and plays dead."

Marge mentions to her favorite bartender that she is thinking of having plastic surgery to enlarge her breasts. The bartender says, "Marge, you don't need surgery to do that. I know how you can do it without surgery."

"Really? How?"

"Just rub toilet paper between them."

"How does that make them bigger?"

"I don't really know . . . but it sure worked for your ass."

ABOUT THE AUTHOR

Michael Lewis is the author/coauthor of eight books
including *Here, There and Everywhere: The 100
Best Beatles Songs* (Black Dog & Leventhal),
The Films of Harrison Ford, and *The Cheapskate's
Guide to Walt Disney World*. He has worked in
the book publishing industry for more than fifteen
years, beginning in sales and marketing and now
as a senior acquisitions/developmental editor at a
major independent publisher. He lives in northern
New Jersey with his wife Amy and daughters
Samantha and Sydney. He doesn't spend much time
in bars these days, but he loves to share jokes with
friends, relatives, and anyone who will listen.

If you've got a joke for consideration in a future
edition of this book, write to Mike in care of his
publisher or e-mail him at SamsPop1@aol.com.